THE LAYMAN'S BIBLE COMMENTARY

THE LAYMAN'S BIBLE COMMENTARY
IN TWENTY-FIVE VOLUMES

THE LAYMAN'S
BIBLE COMMENTARY

Balmer H. Kelly, *Editor*

Donald G. Miller   *Associate Editors*   Arnold B. Rhodes

Dwight M. Chalmers, *Editor, John Knox Press*

VOLUME 19

THE GOSPEL ACCORDING TO
JOHN

Floyd V. Filson

JOHN KNOX PRESS
Atlanta

© M. E. Bratcher 1963

10 9 8 7 6 5 4 3 2

Complete set: ISBN: 0-8042-3086-2
This volume: 0-8042-3079-X
Library of Congress Card Number: 59-10454
First paperback edition 1982
Printed in the United States of America
John Knox Press
Atlanta, Georgia 30365

PREFACE

The LAYMAN'S BIBLE COMMENTARY is based on the conviction that the Bible has the Word of good news for the whole world. The Bible is not the property of a special group. It is not even the property and concern of the Church alone. It is given to the Church for its own life but also to bring God's offer of life to all mankind —wherever there are ears to hear and hearts to respond.

It is this point of view which binds the separate parts of the LAYMAN'S BIBLE COMMENTARY into a unity. There are many volumes and many writers, coming from varied backgrounds, as is the case with the Bible itself. But also as with the Bible there is a unity of purpose and of faith. The purpose is to clarify the situations and language of the Bible that it may be more and more fully understood. The faith is that in the Bible there is essentially one Word, one message of salvation, one gospel.

The LAYMAN'S BIBLE COMMENTARY is designed to be a concise non-technical guide for the layman in personal study of his own Bible. Therefore, no biblical text is printed along with the comment upon it. This commentary will have done its work precisely to the degree in which it moves its readers to take up the Bible for themselves.

The writers have used the Revised Standard Version of the Bible as their basic text. Occasionally they have differed from this translation. Where this is the case they have given their reasons. In the main, no attempt has been made either to justify the wording of the Revised Standard Version or to compare it with other translations.

The objective in this commentary is to provide the most helpful explanation of fundamental matters in simple, up-to-date terms. Exhaustive treatment of subjects has not been undertaken.

In our age knowledge of the Bible is perilously low. At the same time there are signs that many people are longing for help in getting such knowledge. Knowledge of and about the Bible is, of course, not enough. The grace of God and the work of the Holy Spirit are essential to the renewal of life through the Scriptures. It is in the happy confidence that the great hunger for the Word is a sign of God's grace already operating within men, and that the Spirit works most wonderfully where the Word is familiarly known, that this commentary has been written and published.

THE EDITORS AND
THE PUBLISHERS

THE GOSPEL ACCORDING TO

JOHN

INTRODUCTION

The Nature and Purpose of the Gospel According to John

This book is a Gospel. To us it is a familiar kind of book, but in the first century it was a new type of writing, created to express the special nature of the life of Jesus. A Gospel was not content to tell merely the external facts of that life. What counted most was the fact that in Jesus Christ, God was at work in a unique way to bring to sinful men the help they desperately needed. So the Church developed the Gospel as a type of writing that would tell this special kind of story—the story of the life, death, resurrection, and lordship of Jesus Christ as the central work of God for man's redemption.

Mark, it seems, wrote the first Gospel. If we compare the sermon summary of Acts 10:34-43 with the content of Mark, we see that Mark covers the points of the early apostolic preaching and gives in some detail the career and work of the Christ who is the center of that preaching. But there was other such material known to the Church, and the Gospels of Matthew and Luke include much of that additional material; they especially help us by including much teaching which Mark did not include. These three Gospels—which to a great extent have the same outline and material, often in the same wording—are called the Synoptic Gospels. They were written by Christians; they express the faith of the writers; they show the deep loyalty of the Church to Christ; they give to the Church documents which preserve the basic story on which Christian faith must always rest.

The Gospel of John is likewise a Gospel. It speaks of John the Baptist as the forerunner of Jesus; it tells of Jesus' ministry from the time of his baptism to the day of his crucifixion; it witnesses to his resurrection and his gift of the Holy Spirit to his followers; it makes clear the central place of Jesus and the necessity of believing in him; it leaves no doubt that God's central action in all history has occurred in Jesus and that men must answer for their response to this divine offer of life through Christ.

But the Gospel of John is different from the other Gospels. While in broad outline it resembles the Synoptic Gospels, it lacks most of the stories and sayings which they contain. One interpreter has estimated that only eight per cent of the Gospel of John has parallels in the other three Gospels; the rest is new material. This new material is concentrated on a special theme. Instead of telling a great variety of things which Jesus did, and instead of giving his teaching on many subjects, this Gospel focuses attention continuously on the Person of Jesus and his meaning for faith and life.

There can be no doubt about this. The writer, in 20:31, states plainly what his purpose has been; he has made a selection of things Jesus did and has included only a few, which "are written that you may believe that Jesus is the Christ, the Son of God, and that believing you may have life in his name." Thus, instead of talking about the right use of money, duties of children to parents, forgiveness of enemies, and related subjects which the Synoptic Gospels discuss, this Gospel does three things:

1. This Gospel tells who Jesus is. He is "the Christ, the Son of God," the central figure of all history and the effective agent of God's work for men. To bring out the meaning of Jesus for believers, the Gospel gives him many titles: Logos (Word), God, Life, Light, Son, Messiah (Christ), Lord, Son of God, Lamb of God, Rabbi (Teacher), King of Israel, Son of Man. (All of these titles occur in chapter 1.) Many symbolic phrases express how central and indispensable is his work: the Bread of Life; the Light of the World; the Door of the Sheep; the Good Shepherd; the Resurrection and the Life; the Way, the Truth, and the Life; the True Vine. Not only is his unique place made clear throughout the Gospel, but his total work is emphasized. The Son who became incarnate in Jesus has been the Father's active agent in creating and upholding the universe (1:3-5); he has given life to men and sustained them in all their life; he is the Savior and the living Lord, and he will be the Judge of all men. This essential and adequate work of the Christ, the Son of God, reaches from eternity to eternity.

2. This Gospel tells what Jesus offers to men. It sums up the gift in one rich word: Life. Many times it uses the phrase "eternal life" to express the completeness and permanence of the gift

God gives through Christ. The Greek adjective "eternal," derived from a Greek word which has the basic idea of an age or period of time, means "belonging to the age." This can mean "belonging to the coming perfect age," a time when God's people will be with him in blessedness, in contrast to belonging to "the present evil age," as Paul called the present sin-ridden world (Gal. 1:4). But the Gospel of John reflects the New Testament awareness that in the coming and work of Christ the new age has already begun, and it emphasizes the point that by faith in Christ the believer may even now enter into eternal life with God and continue in it for all time to come. So life is a present gift as well as a future privilege. Just what this life is like is not described in detail, but 17:3 makes clear that it is a rich, good, and happy life in loyal relation to God and Christ: "this is eternal life, that they know thee the only true God, and Jesus Christ whom thou hast sent."

3. This Gospel tells how, through the work of Christ, men may receive this eternal life. The way is to "believe that Jesus is the Christ, the Son of God" (20:31); abide in Christ, keep his commandments, and live in love with those who share that faith (15:4, 10, 12). This must be a real faith. It is more than verbal confession; it is more than accepting as true certain statements about Jesus; it is a deep, complete, steady, loyal, obedient commitment of the believer in a life of grateful reverence, worship, and witness. Thus, faith calls for two things: clear-cut and wholehearted decision to believe in Christ and abide in him, and faithful expression of this confession in worship and obedience.

Other Aims of the Writer

In addition to the basic purpose expressed in 20:31, this Gospel was written to make clear other aspects of Christian truth.

1. The Jews, and particularly the Jewish leaders, were completely and tragically wrong in refusing to believe in Jesus as their Christ and Lord. Sometimes it is said that the writer of this Gospel was "anti-Semitic." This is not an accurate statement. In the first place, the Gospel accepts as Scripture the Old Testament, which points to Jesus as its fulfillment. Indeed, Jesus "came to his own home," that is, to Palestine and the Jewish people (1:11), and "salvation is from the Jews" (4:22)—not that the Jews provide it or can give it, but that it came to men in their midst. Jesus

was born a Jew and was "King of Israel" (1:49). His disciples were Jews, and the writer of the Gospel of John, as his way of thinking and his background show, was a Jew. The good news (gospel) is for "whoever believes" (3:16), and this includes Jews. So the writer of this Gospel does not want to exclude Jews from the Church; he wants them to accept Christ and follow him. But he knows that the claim of Christ is important and even crucial for a man's eternal welfare, and he can only regard as wicked the rejection of Jesus by the Jewish leaders and other Jews. He speaks sternly against the Jews, not because he hates them, but because there can be no neutrality concerning Jesus Christ; the people of Israel had the advantage of all that God had done for them through centuries of special opportunity, and so those Jews who rejected the unique privilege which the coming of Jesus offered to them were particularly open to condemnation.

2. To the writer of this Gospel it was important to tell that Jesus presented the gospel message at Jerusalem and especially at the Temple there. In the Synoptic Gospels the ministry of Jesus is located almost entirely in Galilee; in them Jesus comes to Jerusalem only once during his ministry, and then only in the very last days of his earthly life. But in the Gospel of John, Jesus is in Jerusalem for most of the events of the gospel story. A brief period in Cana and Capernaum (2:1-12), another visit to Cana (4:43-54), a stay near the Sea of Galilee and in Galilee (6:1—7:9), and the Resurrection appearance in chapter 21 are the only events which this Gospel locates in Galilee; all the rest (except 4:1-42 in Samaria) take place in or near Jerusalem. Why is this? To the writer of this Gospel it is clear that the real decision for or against the claim of Jesus had to be made at Jerusalem, where the Temple was the center of Jewish life and where the Jewish leaders were concentrated. (Much the same viewpoint led the Twelve, after the resurrection of Jesus, to settle in Jerusalem and refuse to leave, even after Stephen was stoned; see Acts 8:1.)

3. A special concern of the Gospel writer was to show that John the Baptist was only of secondary importance when compared with Jesus. To us it may seem strange for anyone to rank the Baptist above Jesus. Two things could easily have led to that view. In the first place, John the Baptist began his public preaching before Jesus did, and apparently made a tremendous impression by his prophetic message and appeal for repentance. A sec-

ond point is that John baptized Jesus; Jesus thus became, in some sense, a member of John's group, and so could seem to have been merely a disciple of John. Moreover, the movement and reputation of John lived on after his death; months after he died, Jewish leaders did not dare to deny his prophetic call (Mark 11:32), and years later, at Ephesus (where the Gospel of John may have been written), followers of the Baptist were still found (Acts 18: 24—19:7). It seems highly probable that followers of the Baptist were still claiming that John deserved the central place in the life of the Jews; he was the real prophet of God, and Jesus was only a renegade disciple of John. To answer this claim, the Gospel of John emphasizes that the role of the Baptist was preparatory and inferior to that of Jesus (1:6-8, 15; 3:25-30). John knew himself to be merely a "voice," calling people to prepare for the coming of the Lord Jesus (1:23).

4. To some degree the Gospel of John emphasizes the real human life of Jesus. Early in the ancient Church a tendency arose to honor Jesus by denying that he was really human, regarding him as not subject to the limitations and struggles of human life. This view, called Docetism, held that he only "seemed" to be living a human life. Those who held this view meant to honor Christ, but in fact they made of his life a false pretense that could not win men's loyalty. So this Gospel writer states pointedly that "the Word became flesh" (1:14); Jesus' family ties are mentioned (2:12; 7:3, 5); in Samaria "Jesus, wearied as he was with his journey, sat down beside the well" (4:6); and he really died on the cross—it was no pretense (19:34). In many ways this Gospel emphasizes more than the other three the divine nature of Jesus, but it guards against the idea that he was not human.

5. Another purpose of the Gospel writer is to assure Christians that the risen Christ is with them, especially through his sending of the Holy Spirit, or Counselor. Many modern Christians think of Jesus only as a past historical figure. This Gospel clearly presents him as a historical figure who carried out his decisive ministry in Palestine. But this Jesus rose from the dead, was exalted to honor with the Father, and is with his followers in the Church, both by his personal presence (14:23) and by his sending of the Counselor to be with them (15:26; 16:7; in 14:16 and 26 the Spirit is sent by the Father but at Jesus' prompting). Christians have Christ as their present companion; they never have to face life alone.

6. Since Jesus returns to be with his followers, and the Spirit is sent to them to guide them into "all the truth" (16:13), it is not surprising that the Gospel writer emphasizes the growing understanding that Christians may have of the gospel message. During Jesus' earthly life his disciples did not fully understand what was happening; only after his resurrection and the gift of the Holy Spirit did they gain a deeper understanding of what Jesus' coming, works, and words really meant. This fact, noted in 2:22; 12:16; 13:7; and 20:9, helps us to understand the Gospel of John, which is not content merely to report mechanically what Jesus said and did, but rather presents the meaning of that life for men.

7. A minor but not unimportant theme in this Gospel is the repeated reminder that men's unbelief and opposition to God's plan do not surprise God or defeat his purpose. The death of Jesus may seem to frustrate God's plan, but the betrayal by Judas was foretold in Scripture and foreknown by Jesus (6:64; 13:18), and behind the Cross was a divinely fixed "must" which marked it as a part of God's plan for saving men (3:14). The hour at which the central event of history happens is fixed in God's plan (7:6). Those who reject and those who accept Christ are responsible for their decision, but it is God who draws some to him while leaving others untouched by his redeeming power (6:37, 39, 44, 65). The fact of conflict is recognized: the sovereign power of God is above question; the redeeming love of God is central; and the working out of God's purpose is not subject to man's veto but will certainly take place, not perhaps in ways that men can clearly understand, but in ways that faith knows will combine God's wisdom, power, and saving love.

Special Methods Used by the Gospel Writer

To achieve his purposes a writer chooses the methods which he thinks will best serve to win his readers. What methods did the writer of the Gospel of John use to lead men to seek life through faith in Jesus?

1. The writer tells a story. His message is given in a history. Since the writer's real aim is to win people to believe in the risen, living Christ, one might think that the history of the human Jesus was not important. That would be a completely mistaken idea. "The Word became flesh" (1:14). Jesus lived a human life;

it was through his ministry with men, his real death and resurrection, and his continual gift of the Spirit that the gift of life was made available to faith. This Gospel is not a book on systematic theology (valuable as such a book can be), nor an invitation to a mystical experience independent of history; it is the story of a life in which faith can discern God's presence and working for men's salvation.

2. The writer keeps repeating his central point in order to hammer home his message. It is remarkable how few ideas the Gospel contains. Only because we have in mind the many details of the Synoptic Gospels do we fail to see how often this Gospel keeps returning to a few central points: the person of Christ, the need of faith, and the gift of life. Perhaps the best way to see this is to recall how the writer tells who Jesus is. In the first chapter he presents the divine Word, who is the light and life of men; this Word became flesh; he may be called God and the Son of God; he is the Lord, the Lamb of God, the Messiah or Christ, Rabbi, the King of Israel, and the Son of Man. Not all of these titles are repeated in later chapters, but the fact remains that the great titles which the writer wants the reader to connect with Jesus are given in the first chapter and repeated throughout the Gospel. This repetition is the writer's method of making his points. He repeats sayings of Jesus with slight variations. He does not try to make many points, but by repetition he tries to make his points clear, and he implies that these are the central points which the reader needs to learn and remember in order to understand the gospel message.

3. The writer uses the Jewish religious calendar, an annual series of feasts, as the framework of his Gospel, and he usually shows Jesus at Jerusalem to observe these feasts (the exception is 6:4; Jesus does not go to Jerusalem for this Passover). Most prominent of the annual feasts in the Gospel of John is the Passover, which celebrated Israel's deliverance from Egypt and roused hopes of a new deliverance for the Jewish people, now enslaved to Rome. Jesus goes to Jerusalem for a Passover early in his ministry (2:13), feeds the multitude at the time of a second Passover (6:4), and dies at Jerusalem at the time of a third Passover (11:55). (Some think the unnamed feast of 5:1 was a Passover; if so, Jesus' ministry, to include four Passovers, must have lasted over three years; but it is not certain what feast is meant in 5:1.) The importance of the Passover for this Gospel becomes clear in an-

other way: John the Baptist calls Jesus "the Lamb of God, who takes away the sin of the world" (1:29), and Jesus dies on the cross not, as in the other Gospels, after eating the Passover with his disciples, but at the very time the Passover lambs are being slain and prepared for the Passover feast (see 18:28; 19:31). Other Jewish feasts are mentioned. Jesus is at Jerusalem for the unnamed feast of 5:1, for the Feast of Tabernacles (7:2, 10, 14), and for the Feast of Dedication (10:22). Thus in this Gospel, Jesus' ministry and teaching center around the great feasts of the Jewish calendar, mainly in Jerusalem where the religious life of Judaism centers, and for the most part when the maximum number of Jews are present. The Gospel writer wants the reader to realize what Acts 26:26 also says, that "this was not done in a corner."

4. The writer makes continual use of symbolism and describes the work of Jesus by a series of vivid figurative pictures. The Crucifixion, at the time when the Passover lambs were being slain and prepared for the Passover feast (instead of the day after the Passover as in the Synoptic Gospels), was to the writer a symbol of the redemptive effect of the death of Jesus, who saves his people, this time not from political bondage in Egypt, but from the bondage of sin (1:29). Each miracle is to the writer a symbol of the spiritual ministry of Jesus. For example, the healing of the man born blind is a symbol of Jesus' ministry in giving light to the world (8:12; 9:5). Another way of picturing the meaning of that ministry is the series of notable passages beginning "I am . . ." Jesus is described as the Bread of Life (6:35, 48); the Light of the World (8:12; 9:5); the Door of the Sheep (10:7); the Good Shepherd (10:11, 14); the Resurrection and the Life (11:25); the Way, and the Truth, and the Life (14:6); and the True Vine (15:1). These titles describe Jesus and his work in pictures which show what he can do for believers.

5. The writer points to events as "signs" of what Jesus does and, therefore, of who he is. We may think that Jesus made his identity and authority and mission so clear that no one could miss it. But the fact is that most people did miss it. They saw him; they watched him do his kindly acts and mighty deeds; they heard him teach in such fashion that men sent to arrest him returned and told the chief priests and Pharisees, "No man ever spoke like this man!" (7:46). Yet most of his hearers refused to believe in him and follow him. How could this happen? Because in spiritual things

it is never possible to prove authority by outward words and acts. By the very nature of life, faith is a venture—a discernment of truth and a glimpse of God by the eyes of faith. The claim of Christ could not be "proved" as we prove a fact of science. There was a hiddenness about the nature and authority of Christ. He could be and was misunderstood and rejected. But his words and his acts were clues to those whose spiritual eyes were open. His deeds were "signs" that God was present in him with power to save those who sensed the truth and saw the hidden meaning of what he did. The miracles were thus fingers pointing to God's mysterious presence and power at work in his Son (see, for example, 2:11; 4:54; note also 20:30).

6. The writer presents the meaning of the work of Jesus in a series of notable discourses. Connected with almost every event of the ministry of Jesus is teaching which interprets it. And because the one central theme of this Gospel is Jesus Christ and the life he offers to those who believe, in this Gospel Jesus speaks almost entirely about himself and his work. In the discourses he speaks in the "I" form almost continuously. But did Jesus talk only about himself and his claim and work? In the Synoptic Gospels he speaks of many aspects of the life of the disciple and the community. Clearly, then, the Gospel of John ignores much of what Jesus taught and selects the central area of Jesus' teaching for special attention because it was crucial for understanding the gospel. Are these words his literal statements? In the Synoptic Gospels, Jesus really makes the same high claim, but he speaks much more about the Kingdom of God and God's claim on men. In this Gospel we find that the sayings of Jesus, the narrative, and the comments by the author are all in the same literary style. Plainly the writer has expressed Jesus' mind in words of his own choosing. And he has expressed it with an understanding that he fully received only after Jesus' resurrection. In other words, he has blended his interpretation with his report of what Jesus said. As John Calvin wrote, this evangelist "dwells more largely on the doctrine" than do the other three Gospel writers. The words of Jesus in this Gospel concentrate on the central issue, the Person and claim of Jesus, and they do so in a form which reflects both the personal claim of Jesus himself and the interpretation of Jesus developed by the Church and particularly by the writer of the Gospel. Did the writer rightly interpret who Jesus is and what he has done? We have this Gospel in the New Testa-

ment because we find in it the true and necessary interpretation of the Person, ministry, and message of Jesus. He was and is the Christ, the Son of God, and men must believe in him to gain eternal life.

7. The writer places great emphasis on the idea of witness. How can people be awakened to the truth and urgency of the claim made for Jesus? The real meaning of Jesus' life and work is not easily or irresistibly clear to everyone. The author does not expect that all men will see and accept this claim of Christ as they should. But he does emphasize that a strong witness to it has been given in the ministry of both Jesus and the Church. Jesus himself witnesses to the Father (3:32-35). And many witnesses to Jesus are named: the Father (5:32, 37; 8:18); the Scriptures (5: 39); John the Baptist (1:7-8, 15, 32, 34; 3:26; 5:33); Moses (1: 45; 5:46) and the prophets (1:45); Jesus himself (8:18); his works (5:36; 10:25); the crowds who saw a miracle (12:17; they attest the occurrence but not the meaning of it); the disciple at the cross (19:35) and the writer of the Gospel (21:24; perhaps the same disciple as in 19:35); and the Counselor, the Holy Spirit (15:26). In one way or another each of these witnesses can help the sincere reader or listener to sense that in facing Jesus he is dealing with God and his claim on men.

8. The writer frequently uses the dialogue form, in which an inquirer or opponent hears Jesus make an ambiguous statement, misunderstands it, and then receives from Jesus a clearer, more specific teaching. For example, Jesus tells Nicodemus that man must be "born anew" (3:3), or, as the Greek may also mean, "born from above," by the working of God's power. Nicodemus misunderstands Jesus to mean that a man must be physically born a second time. Jesus then makes clear that he was speaking of a complete spiritual (Spirit-caused) renewal of those who respond to him in faith. To understand this Gospel we must be alert for this pattern: a vague or general statement which is misunderstood by the hearer and then clarified by Jesus. The thing to do in studying the Gospel is to watch for the clarifying statement which Jesus gives. That represents his real teaching; it is more important and clear than the vague opening statement of a dialogue.

For Whom Was This Gospel Written?

The Gospel of John exists in Greek and in translations of the

Greek into other languages. It is natural and usual to assume that its author wrote in Greek. A few capable interpreters, however, have argued not only that the writer was a Jew (as is generally agreed), but that he wrote his Gospel in Aramaic, the Semitic language then commonly spoken in Palestine and in certain other Near Eastern areas. The present Greek Gospel of John would thus be a translation from the original Aramaic, which no longer survives.

Why is this claim made? Not merely because the Gospel writer thinks like a Jew and shows knowledge of Palestine and Jewish life; a Greek-speaking Jew could do this. The only solid evidence that the Gospel was originally written in Aramaic would be passages which (1) do not make good sense in the existing Greek Gospel, but (2) can be explained as a faulty translation of an Aramaic original. But the fact is that no such solid ground for this theory has been found. The overwhelming majority of New Testament scholars hold that the Gospel was originally written in Greek.

This conclusion helps us decide who the readers were for whom the Gospel was written. They were people who could read Greek and perhaps only Greek. Were these people Jews? It has been held that the Gospel was written as a missionary book to persuade Jews to believe in Christ. Was it then written for Greek-speaking Palestinian Jews? This is unlikely, since most Jews of Palestine did not read Greek easily. Or was it written to present the gospel message to Greek-speaking Jews who lived in other lands? Possibly. But the chief argument against either of these views is that the Gospel contains little that deals with the special questions, such as the Christian attitude toward Jewish laws and ceremonies, which non-Christian Jewish readers would ask. Moreover, the Gospel is not a pleading invitation to Jews. It does not read like an evangelistic writing directed specifically to Jews; rather, it bluntly condemns Jews for not believing in Jesus. The tone is not what we would expect the writer to use if his special aim were to win his fellow Jews to believe in Jesus as their Christ.

Was the author's purpose, then, to win Gentiles to faith? Possibly this was part of his reason for writing. But again it is remarkable how little the Gospel contains which would suggest that this was the writer's chief concern. He certainly thought that Gentiles belonged in the Church; they as well as the Jews should believe in Jesus as the "Savior of the world" (4:42). But if his main interest was an evangelistic approach to Gentiles, we would expect more pointed references to Gentiles and their needs.

It thus seems most likely that the Gospel was written to help Christians. It had as its purpose the strengthening, deepening, and clarifying of their faith in Jesus as "the Christ, the Son of God" (20:31). It gave a mature statement of the gospel, aimed at helping believers to a fuller and truer faith. The Gospel more than once suggests that there are different levels of faith; a person may believe and yet need a still deeper faith to steady him and protect him from false ideas.

In 2:23-24 "many believed in his name . . . but Jesus did not trust himself to them"; something was lacking in their faith. In 3:2 Nicodemus accepted Jesus as "a teacher come from God," but he never gained the courage and conviction to confess real faith in Jesus (7:51-52). The Samaritans at first believed "because of the woman's testimony," but later believed because of closer touch with Jesus and clearer understanding of who he was (4:39-42). Some followed Jesus because of his "signs" (6:2), and even agreed that he was the coming "prophet" (6:14), but when he made his claim clearer, "many of his disciples drew back" (6:66). Later "many of the people believed in him," but they did not clearly see that he was the Christ (7:31). At one point "many believed in him" (8:30), but as they learned more fully what he claimed to be, they became hostile and were so clearly out of sympathy with him that he finally said, "You are of your father the devil" (8:44). The man born blind, after being healed, at first could confess only that Jesus was "a prophet" (9:17); not until further instructed could he believe in Jesus as the Son of Man and call him "Lord" (9:38). Jesus said that people may believe in his works if they cannot believe in him without such signs (10:38); evidently such belief in his works would be a lesser faith that might lead to a fuller faith in him. Martha could make the very confession that the Gospel was written to promote (compare 11:27 with 20:31), yet in 11:39 her faith was not equal to the test put upon it; she did not believe that the power of Jesus could bring Lazarus back to life. Many Jewish authorities "believed in him" (12:42), but they lacked courage to confess this, and their preference for "the praise of men" (12:43) showed that it was not yet full and clear faith. At the Last Supper, Peter did not understand what Jesus meant by washing the disciples' feet (13:8-9), and his thought and purpose were not steadily firm (13:37-38). Thomas did not know where Jesus was going (14:5); Philip did not understand that Jesus had revealed the Father to them (14:8); the disciples to the end failed to understand Jesus fully, and the Gospel assures us that only after the Resurrection and the gift of the Spirit did they understand truly the words of Scripture and of Jesus (2:22; 12:16; 13:7; 20:9).

The Gospel is thus continually concerned to deepen Christian understanding and faith. Those who believe only in a partial or superficial way must come to a deeper faith; otherwise they will lose touch with Jesus, be intimidated by men's hostility to Christ, be repelled by his full claim, and so in the end lose the great privilege and opportunity that they had begun to accept. This is a Gospel written primarily for Christians. The Greek in 20:31 seems to mean that the readers are to continue in their faith and deepen it by gaining, through the Gospel, a full understanding of who Jesus really is. He is no mere "teacher come from God," no mere "prophet," no mere nationalist Messiah; he is in the fullest sense "the Christ, the Son of God." Readers of the Gospel, by advancing to full and clear faith in him, will enter safely into the eternal life he came to give.

The Author of the Gospel

Most Christian readers have no question about the authorship of this Gospel. In their Bibles the title says that this is "The Gospel According to John." They recognize that this means John the son of Zebedee, one of the twelve Apostles, and they accept him as the author.

How decisive is this title? It is an important guide to what the Church has long believed, but it was not part of the original Gospel. None of our four Gospels names its author, and none of them, when first written, had its present title prefixed to it. When the New Testament Canon began to be formed, toward the middle of the second century, our four Gospels were united in a group, and at that time such titles were needed and were used to distinguish each Gospel from the others. We may be sure that by that time the prevailing view in the Church at large regarded each of these Gospels as written by the person named in its title. So the definite statement that John the Apostle wrote the Fourth

Gospel may be traced back at least to the time this title was prefixed to it in the middle of the second century, and of course may
go back decades earlier, though no such earlier specific direct
testimony has come down to us.

From the time of Irenaeus, who wrote about A.D. 185, the
Johannine authorship has been explicitly and repeatedly asserted
by scholars and leaders of the Church. Irenaeus is quite emphatic
on this point. Perhaps his strongest argument is that as a youth
he heard the aged Polycarp tell of knowing John; thus if Irenaeus
asserts confidently that John was the author of the Fourth Gospel,
he could have been assured of this by Polycarp, a personal disciple of John. Other Christian leaders of the time of Irenaeus
clearly accepted this Gospel as apostolic and authoritative. From
that time to modern days the prevailing view in the Church has
been that the author was John the Apostle.

Later scholars have supported this view with other arguments.
For example, it has been pointed out that Peter and John act together in Luke 22:8 and Acts 3:1, 11; 4:13, 19; 8:14, just as
Peter and the beloved disciple do in John 13:23-24; 20:2-10;
21:7, 20-21; this suggests that the Apostle John was the beloved
disciple who wrote this Gospel.

But though authorship by the Apostle John was asserted in the
title by the middle of the second century, and the Church at
large has held this view from the latter part of the second century,
there was a definite objection to this view at the close of the
second century. The writings of these (few) objectors have not
been preserved, so we cannot study them, but it is significant
that at so late a date there were still leaders in the Church who
refused to accept the tradition that John the son of Zebedee wrote
this Gospel. From what sources did they receive the information
that led them to this conclusion? By what arguments did they
support their view that Cerinthus, or at least someone other than
John, was the author? Possibly such objections arose because the
Fourth Gospel was being used by heretics to support dangerous
ideas, and in particular because the Gospel's teaching about the
Spirit (16:13) was being misused to defend radical new ideas that
would prove fatal to the life and work of the Church. Or possibly
these objectors knew from earlier generations that there was
reason to doubt that John wrote this Gospel. The objections stand
there as a fact which we cannot fully explain.

So from the middle of the second century the Church has generally held that John the son of Zebedee wrote this Gospel, but at the close of the second century there was still some dispute about this view. On the whole, the testimony from the ancient church fathers favors authorship by John the son of Zebedee. In modern times, however, some interpreters prefer to say that a disciple of the Apostle John wrote down John's witness, and that his book was called by John's name because its content and authority came not from John's disciple but from the Apostle John himself.

But the writer of this commentary is held captive by still another possibility, which he must present for study. Suppose that, instead of asking what was said by church writers of the second century and later, we first of all listen to the Gospel itself. Suppose we agree that we can best understand the writer and his relation to Jesus by carefully reading his book. Surely the clues given by statements of the author himself should have much more weight than any later statements about who he was. To let the author speak directly to us, we must ignore the title, for the author did not prefix this title to his Gospel. Let us read the Gospel itself, and ask what its contents tell us about its author.

The first conclusion will be that this Gospel was written by a disciple who lived in or near Jerusalem. Of its twenty-one chapters only about three tell of Jesus' ministry in Galilee; one chapter tells mainly of his visit to Samaria; seventeen deal with his ministry in Jerusalem and nearby regions. This would be strange in a Gospel written by a disciple such as John the son of Zebedee, who lived in Galilee and accompanied Jesus on his extensive ministry in Galilee. But it would be entirely natural in a Gospel written by a disciple who lived in or near Jerusalem. (That John the son of Zebedee had a residence in Jerusalem is only a conclusion drawn from the claim that he wrote this Gospel. There is no evidence for it; to use this inference that John had a Jerusalem residence to support the theory of Johannine authorship is to argue in a circle.)

Does the Gospel itself give any clear clues as to its author? It never names him directly. But in 21:24 it is said that the disciple whom Jesus loved wrote the book. The formal conclusion in 20:30-31 indicates clearly that the Gospel was originally planned and written to end with 20:31. The story was then complete, and 20:30-31 forms a fitting conclusion to a great book. Chapter 21 is thus an appendix, added after the Gospel had been planned and written. But since it is in the same style and has basically the same vocabulary, it is reasonable to argue that it was added very soon after the first twenty chapters were written; and every extant copy of the Gospel contains chapter 21, so it is clear that the Gospel never circulated without this added chapter. The tradition that the beloved disciple wrote the Gospel is thus very early, and it seems rather reasonable to infer that it must come from the circle in which the beloved disciple lived.

Does the Gospel indicate who this beloved disciple was? Yes, it does. It points to Lazarus. Curiously, we get no real help on this question from the first ten chapters. Some have found in 1:41 a veiled reference to John the son of Zebedee. Of the two disciples of John the Baptist who left the Baptist and went to Jesus (1:37), one was Andrew (1:40). The other is not named. Verse 41 says of Andrew that he "first" found his brother Simon and brought him to Jesus. The word "first" appears in two forms in early Greek manuscripts of this Gospel. One form would mean that Andrew was the first to find his brother, and then, it would be implied, the *other* disciple found *his* brother. The only other pair of brothers in the group of disciples were James and John, the sons of Zebedee. So this could mean that at the very beginning of Jesus' ministry John the son of Zebedee was brought into touch with Jesus and in 1:37, 41 is modestly introduced without being named. But the other form of the Greek word for "first" seems better supported by the ancient manuscripts, and it means simply that the first thing Andrew did, before he did anything else, was to bring his brother Simon Peter to Jesus; it thus says nothing about who the other (unnamed) disciple was or what he did. The probable conclusion, then, is that the first ten chapters of the Gospel tell us nothing about the beloved disciple.

Then in chapter 11 we hear of Lazarus. Of all the disciples of Jesus whom this Gospel names, he is the only man of whom it is said that Jesus loved him. And this is said of Lazarus four times: "Lord, he whom you love is ill" (11:3); "Now Jesus loved Martha and her sister and Lazarus" (11:5); "Our friend Lazarus has fallen asleep" (11:11; the Greek word for "friend" has the same root as one Greek word for "love," and it means here "our *beloved friend* Lazarus"); "See how he loved him!" (11:36). These four passages emphasize that Jesus loved Lazarus.

The importance of Lazarus and his sisters in this Gospel has usually been underrated. They hold a climactic place in Jesus' public ministry. At the climax of that ministry, Jesus raises his beloved friend Lazarus from the grave as an acted parable of his ability to give life to those who believe in him. In 11:27 Lazarus' sister Martha makes the very confession which, according to 20:31, the Gospel was written to promote: Jesus is "the Christ, the Son of God" (20:31). The other sister, Mary, anoints Jesus, and Jesus interprets this as a preparation for his burial after his imminent death (12:3, 7). This family of three thus holds the center of attention at the climax of his public ministry; their part in the Gospel leads on to the Last Supper and the story of Jesus' death.

When we come to the last evening of Jesus' earthly life, we find for the first time a reference to the disciple "whom Jesus loved" (13:23). This particular way of referring to a disciple without giving his name is never found before that last evening. It occurs again in 19:26-27, where Jesus commits his mother to the care of the beloved disciple and that disciple "took her to his own home," presumably in or near Jerusalem (Bethany, the home of Lazarus, was near Jerusalem; 11:18). It occurs again in 20:2-10, where Peter and the beloved disciple run to the grave of Jesus and find it empty. Finally, it occurs again in 21:7, 20-23, where the beloved disciple recognizes the risen Jesus, and Jesus refuses to say anything about what will happen to the beloved disciple.

If we ask who this beloved disciple was, and let the Gospel writer suggest the answer, only Lazarus will come to mind. Four times in chapter 11 Lazarus has been described in a way which shows that Jesus had a special love for him. No other disciple has been so described. Lazarus has been at a supper with Jesus (12:2). Lazarus is so important that he alone of the disciples has been marked out by the Jewish leaders to be put to death (12:9-11). So when we read in chapter 13 that the beloved disciple is reclining with Jesus (as Lazarus did in chapter 12) and that Jesus loved this disciple, as chapter 11 has said four times that he loved Lazarus, the natural inference is that Lazarus is the beloved disciple. Lazarus lived in Bethany, just outside of Jerusalem to the east, on the southeastern slope of the Mount of Olives, and "from that hour" he could take the mother of Jesus from the crucifixion site to his home (19:27). Lazarus had been raised from the dead; he knew the life-giving power of Jesus; he particularly would be alive to the possibility of the resurrection of

Jesus. It is not surprising, then, that he was the first to recognize at the empty tomb that Jesus had risen (20:8) and to recognize the risen Jesus by the Sea of Galilee (21:7). Of Lazarus, since he had already died and been raised, the rumor could most easily arise that he would not die before the Lord came (21:23).

In all of these ways Lazarus fits the situation of the beloved disciple, and if we consider the Fourth Gospel by itself, the natural conclusion is that the author means us to see in Lazarus the beloved disciple. Otherwise the Gospel would break in two after chapter 12. In chapters 11 and 12 we would have Lazarus as Jesus' beloved disciple, a member of a prominent family, whose acts and words express the central theme of the Gospel, life through Christ; then suddenly in chapter 13 we would have to forget that Jesus had a special love for Lazarus, and begin to think of some other completely unidentified beloved disciple. This would be a jarring way to write; it would make an awkward break at the climax of Jesus' public ministry. The Gospel moves on in unity and clarity, without misleading the reader, only if we accept the clear clues and say that Lazarus was the beloved disciple.

Then, if we follow 21:24, we must say that Lazarus was in some sense the author of the Gospel. Since 21:23 implies that he had died when that verse was written (see comment on 21:23), we may say one of three things: (1) Lazarus wrote chapters 1-20 and his friends ("we" in 21:24) added chapter 21 after his death. (2) Some friend or assistant of Lazarus, writing in his name, wrote the entire Gospel in two stages: first, chapters 1-20 during the lifetime of Lazarus, and then chapter 21 at some time after his death. (3) If we take seriously the hint of 12:10 that Lazarus became a martyr for Christ, we probably should assume that he died in the early years of the Apostolic Church. Then we may say that some faithful Jerusalem-centered friend of the beloved disciple Lazarus, writing in the name of Lazarus, perhaps some years after Lazarus had died, wrote chapters 1-20, while chapter 21 was added still later by someone else, perhaps after the Church was no longer clear about the beloved disciple's true identity and had begun to identify him with John the son of Zebedee.

Many Christians will find it hard to accept this identification of Lazarus as the beloved disciple. They will think it strange that the ancient Church did not say anything to support this view. They will wonder how the view that John the Apostle was the beloved disciple arose if actually Lazarus was the beloved disciple. They will consider it more reasonable to follow the testimony of the ancient church fathers and say that John the Apostle wrote the Fourth Gospel. To the present writer the testimony of the Gospel itself must be given the decisive role, and it seems to point definitely to Lazarus as the beloved disciple. This view, like the alternate views, cannot answer all of the questions we may ask, but it lets the Gospel speak for itself.

Whatever view of authorship we adopt, however, two solid facts must not be lost from sight. This Gospel is Jerusalem-centered, and it combines the story of Jesus' earthly career with the early Christian interpretation of what that career means for Christian faith. It is this combination of Jerusalem-centered historical report and mature Christian interpretation which is characteristic of this Gospel.

The fact that the Gospel author blended historical fact and mature interpretation makes the task of a commentator difficult. If the commentator keeps trying to distinguish just what Jesus said and did, and just what the author has added, he fails in two respects to fulfill his task: (1) He can never separate neatly the literal words and acts of Jesus from the author's Christian interpretation, because the two are continuous and inextricably blended. (2) If the commentator constantly tries to separate the two, he distracts attention from a clear and persuasive statement of what the Gospel writer himself wanted men to hear. And the first duty of a commentator is to let the Gospel writer's message speak clearly to the reader of the commentary. If, on the other hand, the commentator concentrates solely on clear statement of the Gospel writer's mind, he can be criticized for failing to make the modern Christian see that the Gospel is not mere literal report but is a rich interpretation of what Jesus said and did.

What shall the commentator do? His first task is to state and explain the Gospel writer's meaning. But he must insert again and again brief references to the other Gospels and to the situation of Jesus himself, so that the reader will not forget that this masterly Gospel is outstanding in the world's literature precisely because it is a powerful and essentially true interpretation of the central life of world history. We must hear first and mainly what the Gospel writer wants to say to us. We must also let him point us back to the historical figure, whose own historical career we can understand adequately only by intensive study of the other three Gospels, with their somewhat more literal report of what Jesus said and did.

The Date and Place of Writing

None of our Gospels can be dated with certainty, and we do not need to know the exact year in which each was written. If the Gospel of John had been written in Aramaic, it most probably would have been written in Palestine or Syria, and its date would have been fairly early in the history of the Church, perhaps between A.D. 60 and 75. But if we accept as almost certain that this Gospel was originally written in Greek, it is more difficult to determine its date and place of origin. It is most often thought to have been written in Asia Minor, in or near Ephesus, toward the end of the first century. This would agree with the ancient tradition that John the son of Zebedee wrote the Gospel at Ephesus in his old age, after the other Gospels had been written. If John or a disciple of his wrote the Gospel, a date late in the first century fits well (the poorly attested ancient tradition that the Apostle John was martyred by the Jews earlier in the first century may safely be rejected). If we take seriously the theory that Lazarus wrote the Gospel, it may well have been written in Palestine, or in any other place where he or his friends went to teach, and the date would probably be several decades before the end of the first century.

Some decades ago a few interpreters wanted to date the Gospel as late as the early or middle years of the second century. More recently, however, a papyrus fragment of the Gospel dating about A.D. 130, or possibly earlier, has been found in Egypt. A so-called "unknown gospel" of about the same date has been found, and its author seems to have used material from the Fourth Gospel, which therefore must have been written before this "unknown gospel" was. Clearly the Gospel of John must have been written not later than the very early years of the second century, and most probably the latest possible date would be A.D. 90-100. But it must be remembered that no matter who wrote the Gospel, it could have been written many years before that decade, especially if we decide, as many are now inclined to do, that its author did not know or depend on any of the Synoptic Gospels. The discovery of early papyri of John in Egypt has raised the question whether this Gospel may have been written in Egypt rather than Ephesus. Origin in Egypt is not impossible, just as origin in Palestine or Syria is not impossible. But early echoes of this Gospel in Christian writers of western Asia Minor show that it was written in the Ephesus region or was brought there and received with approval shortly after it was written.

OUTLINE

The Eternal Divine Word, the Son of God, Incarnate in Jesus Christ, the Lamb of God. John 1:1-51

Prologue: The Eternal Divine Word Became Flesh (1:1-18)
The First Witnesses to Jesus (1:19-51)

Jesus' Public Ministry. John 2:1—12:50

The Gift of New Life to Israel and All Men (2:1—4:54)
Jesus' Ministry Met by Both Faith and Unbelief (5:1—12:50)

Jesus' Final Ministry to His Faithful Followers. John 13:1—17:26

The Footwashing Teaches Mutual Humble Love (13:1-38)
Farewell Promises and Teaching (14:1—16:33)
Jesus Prays for Himself and His Disciples (17:1-26)

The Glory and Victory of Jesus Revealed in His Death and Resurrection. John 18:1—20:29

The Betrayal and Arrest of Jesus (18:1-11)
The Condemnation of Jesus (18:12—19:16)
The King of the Jews Crucified and Buried (19:17-42)
The Resurrection and the Gift of the Holy Spirit (20:1-29)

The Purpose of the Gospel. John 20:30-31

Another Resurrection Appearance. John 21:1-25

The Third Appearance to the Disciples (21:1-14)
Peter's Ministry and Martyrdom (21:15-19)
The Role of the Beloved Disciple (21:20-24)
Conclusion (21:25)

COMMENTARY

THE ETERNAL DIVINE WORD, THE SON OF GOD, INCARNATE IN JESUS CHRIST, THE LAMB OF GOD

John 1:1-51

Prologue: The Eternal Divine Word Became Flesh (1:1-18)

The purpose of this Gospel is to lead the readers to whole-hearted faith in Jesus as the Christ, the Son of God (20:31). The Prologue sets the stage; it gives a background to help us understand who Jesus Christ is, what his total work is, and how his earthly life fits into the entire history of God's work for men. The writer does not belittle the earthly life of Jesus; he writes his Gospel to tell the story of that life, and it is essential to his message that Jesus lived a real human life (vs. 14). But first the reader needs to catch a glimpse of its setting and divine origin.

To relate the life of Jesus to the life and total work of God, the writer chooses a familiar term, "the Word" (vss. 1, 14). This term had an Old Testament background, for the Old Testament describes the power and vitality of the Word of God (Gen. 1:3, 9; Ps. 33:6). It was familiar in later Jewish thought. The apocryphal book, the Wisdom of Solomon, written in Greek just before or during Jesus' lifetime, says that God by his Word created all things, heals all men, and sends his commands to men. Philo of Alexandria, a contemporary of Jesus, speaks of the Word as the image of God, and even as a second God, by whom God created the world. The term was also familiar both in Greek philosophy (especially Stoicism) and in popular Hellenistic thought. Thus "the Word" was widely used to refer to the active divine agent through whom God makes, sustains, and directs the world and man. (In I Corinthians 8:6 this divine agent is called the "Lord, Jesus Christ"; in Colossians 1:13-20 and Hebrews 1:1-3 he is called the "Son.") The Gospel writer takes up and uses this widely known idea of the Word as the active divine agent of God. This active agent, he says, entered history in a real person who lived a real human life, made the Father known to men, and provided for them the way to eternal life. The Gospel uses the idea of "the Word" only in this Prologue. Once the personal name of Jesus Christ has been introduced (vs. 17), the Gospel speaks no more of the Word in this special sense; it talks only of the person Jesus. Even in the Prologue the writer is not satisfied to refer only to the Word. He adds other titles; he calls the Word not only "God" (vs. 1) but also "light" (vss. 4-5, 8-9), "life" (vs. 4), and "Son" (vss. 14, 18). No title is too high for Jesus Christ; no one title can express all that his coming has meant.

Verses 1-5 tell what the divine Word had done at the Creation and in the previous history of the world. These verses do not yet speak of the unique coming of the Word into human life; verse 14 comes explicitly to that point. The Word already existed "in the beginning" (see Gen. 1:1), when the world was created. At that first moment of time the Word existed "with God." He was one in nature with God. This does not deny that in God we can distinguish between the Father and the Son, but the oneness of the Word with God is so real and close that the Word can be described as God (see also 20:28). Repetition for emphasis is characteristic of this Gospel; verse 2 repeats the fact that this Word was present "in the beginning with God." He was present, however, not in a passive way, but as the active agent through whom God made all things (vs. 3; see Col. 1:16; Heb. 1:2). The Word—or, as he is later called, the Son—has life in himself (5:26), and it is by his life-giving action that all living things come into being (1:4; 5:21).

This divine life of the Word is "the light of men" (vs. 4); understanding and moral insight, mind and spiritual vision, come to men by God's creation through the working of the living Word. This divine Light "shines in the darkness" of ignorance and sin and offers light on life's way. Here a dark note enters the picture: the darkness in verse 5 is more than absence of light; it is an active rejection of God's will, a hostile darkness that opposes the working of the divine Light. But the darkness of evil "has not overcome" the Light, which continues its active work. (The Greek could be translated, "The darkness has not *understood* it," but the Greek verb here seems rather to mean "overcome." Throughout the Gospel, darkness is not mere absence of spiritual light; it is the realm of active hostility to God, to the Light, and to believers in Jesus.)

After the general statement that the Word created all things and has given life and light to men through the centuries, the Prologue speaks of John the Baptist. The references to John here (and in verses 15, 19-36; 3:23-30) emphasize how important it is to understand correctly the relation of John to Jesus. Perhaps the writer had once been a disciple of John and wanted his readers to understand why he had left John to follow Jesus. Perhaps exaggerated claims were being made for John and the writer wanted to correct them (note the later influence of John at Ephesus as reported in Acts 18:25; 19:3). John was a good and important man, sent from God to bear witness to the Light, or Word. The divine purpose in sending John was that through John's testimony to the Light all might believe in the Light. No matter what claims others might make for John, he was not the Light. His role was subordinate; he pointed men to the Light. Men should believe in the Light.

This Light did more than shine (vs. 5). He enlightened the spirit, mind, and heart of every man. In verses 9-13 the thought that this Light or Word became flesh hovers in the mind of the writer, but he does not clearly say this until verse 14; verses 9-13, especially verses 9-10, still include the idea of verses 4-5—that the Light revealed God and illuminated men during the Old Testament period. This Light was always in the world he had made; he was always illuminating all men; yet, because of the hostile darkness (vs. 5) and the sin of those very men (vs. 29), the world did not recognize the Light and acknowledge its obligation to him. In particular, he came to Israel; "his own home" could mean the world, but probably refers here to Palestine as the home of God's Chosen People, who should have been quick to welcome and believe in the Light. But his own people Israel did not give him their faith and loyalty. Verse 11 sounds as if none received him. This Gospel many times says something in an absolute way, as if there were no exceptions, and then goes on at once to say that there were exceptions. So here, verse 12 goes on to say, some did receive him. It is implied that they were a minority, but they "received him," that is, "believed in his name"; and to them he gave the gift of life, "power to become children of God." Real life, real sonship with God, thus comes not by physical creation but, as 3:3 says, by rebirth, by a complete and radical renewal of sinful man. This new life, this rebirth, is not man's doing; these children of God are born into eternal life with God not by physical descent ("blood") or physical love ("the flesh," "the will of man"), but only by the redeeming and creative action of God through the Word, the Light, the Son (vs. 13). In this Gospel, sonship is not a natural privilege of all men but a miraculous creation and gift which God gives through his Son.

How this happened is now told in more explicit words. The divine Word, always active in creating, upholding, and enlightening God's world, became flesh and lived among men (vs. 14). He was full of the divine grace which actively reached out to save men in their need. He was full of the divine truth and integrity; he was entirely free from any false thought or motive or way of action. He dwelt "among us," and "we have beheld his glory." Who were the "we"? All men? The Jews? The Christians in the days of his ministry? The Apostles? The writer (editorial "we")? Probably "we" refers to the eyewitnesses of Jesus' life; they saw by faith that he was the divine Word, the Light, the Son of God, and so they discerned in this human form the divine glory (the divine greatness and splendor) that found its expression in Jesus' love and redemptive work for men. The writer seems to class himself among the eyewitnesses; but the "we" reminds the reader that others besides the writer could give the same testimony. We must beware of thinking that the vision and the glory here described were visible to indifferent and hostile people. This Gospel makes it clear that men could see Jesus and his deeds with the physical eye and still miss the fact that God was uniquely and powerfully present in him to save men. His glory was a hidden glory, which only the eye of faith could see; because it was expressed in humility of life and without parade, it could be missed, although clues and hints were there for those who were spiritually alert.

To the Gospel writer the essential role of John the Baptist was to identify and bear witness to Jesus (see 1:6-8, 19-36; 3:23-30). Verse 15 interrupts the testimony of believing followers of Jesus to repeat John's testimony. He is quoted as repeating a testimony that he had given after Jesus' ministry had begun. John had said, according to verse 15, that while Jesus "comes after me"— that is, Jesus began his ministry after John began his—yet Jesus "ranks before me"; that is, he ranks above John and his movement supersedes that of John, and rightly so, for this incarnate

Word existed before John was born. By his very nature as the eternal divine Word and Light of men he ranks far above John, whose task it was to urge men to believe in the incarnate Word.

In verse 16 the writer returns to the eyewitness testimony which he and other believing followers of Jesus can give. The incarnate Word, full of grace and truth (vs. 14), fully divine (vs. 1), has brought the divine grace to men, and these believing witnesses can testify that in him they have found richly available the "fullness" of divine grace. "Grace upon grace" means that they have received grace in a continual succession of undeserved gifts. Here we see the very nature of the gospel. It is not a new law. God gave the Law through Moses (vs. 17), and this Gospel does not despise the Law. But the Law does not save; it cannot lay bare the deepest truth about God's doings and man's need and God's gracious answer to it. That active saving grace, that revealing, guiding, active truth, came through Jesus Christ, who fulfilled the hopes of Israel (see 1:41).

Through this historical Jesus, God has become known to men in a way adequate for their salvation. "No one has ever seen God" (vs. 18); men had had visions of God, as the Old Testament reports (for example, Isa. 6:1), but such ancient visions did not make known his nature and his work in a way that would truly redeem men and give them eternal life. The one adequate revelation of God—the one real appearance of God to make known to men his nature, will, grace, and demand—occurred in Jesus Christ. Verse 18 calls him "the only Son" (see 1:14; 3:16); others become children of God by the work and gift of Christ and are not sons in the same sense that Jesus is. Some Greek manuscripts read here "the only God" instead of "the only Son," and, as 1:1 and 20:28 show, to this writer Jesus Christ, the Word made flesh, could be called God. It is possible that the author wrote his Prologue to describe the Word as God in verse 1 and Jesus Christ as the only God in verse 18; but probably in verse 18 as in verse 14 he spoke of Jesus as "the only Son," who alone has adequately revealed God and given God's grace to men.

The First Witnesses to Jesus (1:19-51)

The entire Gospel is a witness to Jesus as "the Christ, the Son of God" (20:31). The author writes not to attract attention to himself but to point to Jesus and lead men to put their faith in him. The importance of a clear witness to Jesus is stated even in the Prologue; God sent John the Baptist "to bear witness to the light," and John was content to take a lesser role and guide all men to look to Jesus for light and help (1:6-8, 15) Now, before telling the story of Jesus' public ministry, the Gospel reports more explicitly what John testified concerning Jesus, and adds the witness of Andrew, Philip, and Nathanael.

John the Baptist: Jesus Is the Lamb of God (1:19-34)

When the story begins, John had been preaching and baptizing for some time on the east side of the Jordan River (vs. 28). Word of his powerful preaching had reached the religious leaders in Jerusalem. "The Jews" of verse 19 seems to be the Sanhedrin, the highest ruling body of the Jewish faith, composed of priests (Sadducees) and Pharisees. In that body the Pharisees were influential, and verse 24 indicates that it was they who decided that John's stirring preaching must be investigated to keep him from misleading the Jewish people. So the leaders sent a delegation of "priests and Levites" to question John: "Who are you?" They knew his name; they wanted to learn what authority he had to carry on an independent preaching ministry. Was he a prophet? Did he claim to be the expected Messiah? ("Christ." The word "Messiah" comes from the Hebrew language; both words mean "anointed." The term here refers to the great anointed leader promised to Israel and expected by great numbers of Israelites.)

John made no special claim for himself. He said that he was not the expected Christ (vs. 20). Malachi 4:5 had promised that God would again send the fiery prophet Elijah to Israel before the coming of the final day of the Lord. John, when asked, denied that he fulfilled this promise. (In the other Gospels, it is clear from the way the writers describe John's clothing and food that they think he did fulfill Malachi 4:5; in Matthew 17:11-13 and Mark 9:12-13, Jesus identifies John as Elijah.) John also denied that he was the expected prophet like Moses whom, according to Deuteronomy 18:15, 18, God had promised to send to speak for him and to lead Israel.

But John spoke with a note of authority. The delegation from Jerusalem asked why; by what right had he stepped into the role of the most stirring preacher of his day? They needed an answer to report to the religious leaders of Israel at Jerusalem (vs. 22). In reply John quoted Isaiah 40:3. (Matthew 3:3; Mark 1:3; and

Luke 3:4 apply the verse to John, but here John himself quotes it.) The original meaning of the verse was that a messenger of God was calling for the preparation of a straight, smooth highway through the wilderness so that the exiles in Babylonia could have a direct, easy journey back to their home in Palestine. The Gospels use the words to describe John as preparing for the appearance of Jesus (who here is called "the Lord"; see 20:28). This is the only aspect of John's ministry which is given in all four Gospels. Other Gospels speak also of his social message (Luke) and of his independent prophetic appeal for righteousness; in the Gospel of John only this preparatory aspect of the Baptist's work is mentioned, and it is John himself who emphasizes it. John prepares the way for Jesus the Lord and witnesses to him. John is only a voice; he wants no personal credit or honor; he directs attention to the Greater One who is ready to appear. Verses 24-28 do this still more explicitly.

The messengers from Jerusalem rightly point out that John is more than just a voice. He is baptizing (vs. 25); he is gathering a group united in loyalty to himself and his message. The messengers see that for John to baptize is to set a group apart for some purpose. Why is he baptizing? If he were the Christ or Elijah or the Prophet they would understand why, but since he makes no personal claim for himself they ask why he baptizes and gathers a group of disciples (1:35; 3:25). He replies that his role is minor and temporary. He baptizes, but only with water (vs. 26). The act is preparatory for another baptism, baptism with the Holy Spirit (vs. 33). That greater baptism John cannot give. But the One who can is already present. He stands among John's listeners; no one recognizes him yet for what he really is, but he is there, and he "comes after" John in the sense that he takes up his ministry after John has been preaching and baptizing for some time. He is far greater than John, who says that he is not good enough even to untie the sandal thong of the Greater One who is ready to begin his ministry (vs. 27).

The Gospel of John gives a number of place names not found in the other Gospels. These references to specific places show knowledge of Palestine. But we do not now know the location of some of these places. This "Bethany beyond the Jordan" (vs. 28) probably was on or near the east bank of the Jordan River, but we do not know exactly where it was located. Probably it was not a city but an unimportant place near the east end of a

ford over the Jordan. It was accessible to visitors from the west side
of the Jordan and was suitable as a place for baptism. The Gospel
notes that it was "beyond the Jordan," that is, on the east side of
that river. It is so described to distinguish it from the Bethany near
Jerusalem (11:1).

The next day John identified Jesus (vs. 29). To the messengers
John had said only that the Greater One stood among them (vs.
26; as vss. 32-34 indicate, John had already baptized Jesus). But
the next day, when Jesus approached, John identified him as "the
Lamb of God, who takes away the sin of the world." Did the
Gospel writer have in mind the fact that, according to 18:28 and
19:14, Jesus would die at the very hour the Passover lambs were
being slain and prepared for the Passover feast? Strictly speaking,
the Passover lamb was not an offering for sin, but the Early
Church very likely saw some such connection, combining in
thought the Passover lamb, the sacrifices for sin in the Book of
Leviticus, and the Suffering Servant who, like a lamb led to the
slaughter, bore the sin of many (Isa. 53:7, 12). The Gospel of
John sees this death as a saving act, not just for Israel but for the
world (1:29; 3:16; 4:42). Verse 30 recalls verse 15: Jesus came
to public attention later than John did, but then he quickly out-
ranked John, because his ministry was not merely that of a man
whose life began with his human birth; as the divine Son or Word
he existed in the infinite reaches of time back before John was
born (see 8:58), and in him God was uniquely present and active
to save men.

The other Gospels tell that John baptized many people who
repented, and so prepared them for the coming Kingdom and its
Leader. But the Gospel of John mentions only one purpose of
John's baptism: it enables John to identify for Israel that Greater
One who was to come after him and outrank him (vss. 30-31).
John had not known who was to have that unique role, but he
had been told in some way by God that he would see the Spirit
of God descend like a dove (in the form of a dove?) and remain
on the person who was to be men's Lord (vs. 33). This he saw
happen when Jesus was baptized (vss. 32, 34). John does not
actually say that he baptized Jesus, but he implies that he did.
When he saw the Spirit descend upon Jesus, he knew that Jesus
was the Expected One. The paragraph uses three noteworthy titles
to describe Jesus: "the Lamb of God, who takes away the sin of
the world," "he who baptizes with the Holy Spirit," and "the Son

of God" (vss. 29, 33, 34). It is important to note that water baptism was only preparatory; it was not the real Christian baptism. The real Christian baptism was the baptism with the Holy Spirit which Jesus was to perform (and began to perform in 20:22).

Andrew: Jesus Is the Messiah (1:35-42)

Verses 35-51 tell of the first disciples of Jesus and report the witness which three of them gave to him. The day after the witness of verses 29-34, while John was standing with two of his disciples (vs. 35), he saw Jesus walking nearby and repeated his testimony, already recorded in verse 29, that Jesus was the Lamb of God (vs. 36). This meant, as the two disciples understood, that Jesus, not John, was the central figure in God's plan. So they left John and followed Jesus (vs. 37). He realized that he was being followed, and turned and asked them what they wanted (vs. 38). They called him "Rabbi," the Jewish word for Teacher (literally, "My Teacher"), and asked Jesus where he was staying (vs. 28 shows that they were at Bethany beyond Jordan). On his invitation, they went to his lodging place and talked with him from about four in the afternoon to the end of the day (vs. 39). One of these two men is not named; he is traditionally thought to be John the son of Zebedee, but the passage does not indicate this. The other was Andrew, brother of Simon Peter (vs. 40).

The first thing Andrew did was to find Simon, who apparently was also at Bethany beyond Jordan, where the Baptist was preaching and baptizing, and so presumably was also a disciple of John the Baptist. Andrew told Simon what he and his unnamed companion had learned from their talk with Jesus. The Baptist's witness and their own talk with Jesus had convinced them that Jesus was the Messiah (vs. 41; see comment on 1:19-34). Andrew's aim was to guide his brother to believe in Jesus as the Christ. When he took Simon to Jesus (vs. 42), Jesus with penetrating look discerned Simon's readiness to believe and his capacity to serve, and gave him a new name to express his great possibilities for steady leadership. He called him "Cephas." This Aramaic word was identical in meaning with the Greek name Peter; both mean "Rock." Jesus called Simon "Mr. Rock." This was no playful joke. Jesus was not teasing Peter because he was unsteady and was certain to deny his Lord under trial; the new name was a serious forecast that Peter would prove to be, as the

early chapters of Acts show us he actually was, the strong, coura-
geous, steady leader of the Early Church.

Philip and Nathanael: Jesus Is the Promised Divine King of Israel (1:43-51)

On the next day Jesus decided to leave John the Baptist. He
had begun to win disciples and was ready to begin to act independently. He determined to go first to Galilee (vs. 43). But before
leaving he found Philip, a native of Bethsaida, a city located on
the north shore of the Sea of Galilee just east of where the Jordan
River flows into that sea. He asked Philip to go back to Galilee
with him. Though the other Gospels know of a house of Peter
and Andrew (Mark 1:29) at Capernaum, here Andrew and Peter,
like Philip, were from Bethsaida. This could explain how Jesus
first met Philip; through his newly won disciples, Andrew and
Peter, he met their friend and fellow townsman Philip and invited Philip to become his disciple. Philip evidently agreed at
once to go with Jesus.

But Philip did more. He found Nathanael (vs. 45), a man of
Cana in Galilee, as 21:2 tells. At that time Jesus was not in Gali-
lee but was near John the Baptist on the lower Jordan, consider-
ably south of Galilee. Yet all of these first disciples were from
Galilee. This indicates how widely the interest in the Baptist had
spread and how deeply the reports of John's preaching had stirred
Galilee. Philip told Nathanael that Jesus of Nazareth was the ex-
pected leader of Israel, whose coming had been announced by
Moses (the traditional author of the Pentateuch; see Gen. 49:10;
Deut. 18:15) and by the prophets.

Nathanael, who lived in Cana, nine miles north of Nazareth,
thought of Nazareth only as a small and unimportant town, and
asked whether anything good could come from such a place (vs.
46). Could God find his unique leader for Israel in so unpromis-
ing a town? Philip challenged Nathanael to come and see for himself, so he went with Philip to see Jesus. As he approached, Jesus,
with unrivaled capacity to discern the true character of those he
met, described him as "an Israelite indeed," a worthy member of
God's people and free from guile and deception (vs. 47). Nathanael was skeptical about whether Jesus could understand him
without previously knowing him, but Jesus showed that he knew
things which happened where he was not present; he had seen
Nathanael sitting under a certain fig tree just before Philip asked

him to come and see Jesus (vs. 48). This unique knowledge of men and their doings convinced Nathanael. He called Jesus not only "Rabbi" (Teacher; see vs. 38), but also "Son of God" and "King of Israel" (vs. 49). By these titles he agreed that Jesus was, as Andrew had said (vs. 41) and Philip had implied (vs. 45), the expected God-sent Christ and the rightful leader of Israel. In reply Jesus promised that Nathanael would see greater things than this ability to see him under the fig tree (vs. 50); he would see heaven opened and the angels of God ascending and descending upon the Son of Man (vs. 51; compare the vision of Jacob in Gen. 28:12-13).

In using the title "Son of man" (Jesus' favorite self-designation in all four Gospels), Jesus described himself as a person of heavenly origin who also shared in and truly represented human life. He promised to provide for believers continual contact between heaven and earth, between God and man. The unceasing movements of the angels symbolized this continuous tie with God, this constant access to divine help open to all who would believe in Jesus as the divine Son of Man. He who knows Jesus as the Son of Man, the Christ, the Son of God, knows the Father; he has the gift of life and continual divine help in every need.

JESUS' PUBLIC MINISTRY
John 2:1—12:50

The Gift of New Life to Israel and All Men (2:1—4:54)

The Power of Jesus to Give New Life (2:1-25)

On the third day after the conversation with Nathanael (1:47-51), Jesus had reached Galilee, where he visited two cities: Cana (vs. 1) and Capernaum (vs. 12). Probably he went to Cana because he and his mother knew the family celebrating a marriage, and Jesus and his disciples were included in the invitation (vs. 2). Perhaps also Nathanael, whose home was in Cana (21:2), had invited Jesus to visit his home there. The disciples who went with Jesus included Philip and Nathanael, probably Andrew and Peter, and perhaps others not mentioned in chapter 1.

It was the custom to serve wine to the guests at such a celebration. On this occasion the supply of wine ran out (vs. 3). Mary

the mother of Jesus learned promptly of the host's embarrassment; this hints that she was well acquainted in that home. Her
report to Jesus was an implicit request to him to help the embar-
rassed host. His reply (vs. 4) was not disrespectful; in Greek the
word for "O woman" carries no note of disrespect or coarseness.
But Jesus did avoid using the word for "mother," and he implied
that in his ministry he would never do anything merely because
others wanted him to do it—not even for his mother. He would
always act in obedience to God. His life had a divine plan; for
each stage in it there was an "hour." In this Gospel, "hour" is a
key word; it almost always means the predestined hour of Jesus'
death, but here it may refer to the hour or time when it was
God's will for him to meet this host's crisis. He had to act according to the divine plan, and not at any other person's direction or
suggestion. His mother accepted this reply. Jesus must follow his
own way; but she expressed faith in his power and willingness to
help when she told the servants to do whatever Jesus ordered (vs.
5). That she could direct the servants shows again that she was
well acquainted in that home.

The six large jars (vs. 6) probably had provided water for the
guests at the wedding feast to use in the ceremonial washings prescribed by Jewish tradition. Since they seem to have been empty
or nearly so, the feast must have been going on for some time
when the wine ran out. Somewhere near at hand was a plentiful
supply of water, from either wells or springs (as at the modern
Kefr Kenna, possibly the location of ancient Cana, four miles
northeast of Nazareth) or from cisterns (such as have been found
at Khirbet Kana, nine miles north of Nazareth; Khirbet Kana is
the more probable location of ancient Cana). At Jesus' direction,
the servants filled the six jars to the brim with water (vs. 7). Then
at his command (vs. 8) some of the liquid was drawn from one
of the jars and given to the guest who was master of ceremonies
or toastmaster. This man, not knowing what had happened, called
the bridegroom and said that this was the best wine of the feast
(vss. 9-10). The usual custom was to serve the best wine first, and
then, when much drinking had dulled the drinkers' senses, the
poorer wine; the toastmaster thought that this bridegroom had
reversed the usual practice. This is the Gospel's way of attesting
that the water had really been changed into wine of the best qual-
ity; Jesus had made available to the host a supply of something between 120 and 180 gallons of good wine.

This miracle, the writer adds, was the first sign Jesus did (vs. 11). "Sign," another key word in this Gospel, refers to a remarkable deed in which eyes of faith can see God's presence and power at work in Jesus to attest his divine nature and mission. The sign manifested Jesus' glory to those with eyes of faith; "glory," another key word, means Jesus' unique divine nature and splendor which rightly claims men's reverence and loyalty. The disciples present at the marriage feast "believed in him." They already had begun to believe in him (1:41, 45, 49), but their faith became deeper and firmer when they saw this striking manifestation of God's presence and power in Jesus.

For the Gospel writer this miracle, like those in later chapters, had a symbolic meaning. Into the inadequate or insipid religious life which Jesus found among his people, he brought the active ferment of a new message and power. That the old way was now surpassed by a new way of salvation is further emphasized in 2: 13-22, which declares the Temple antiquated by Jesus' death and resurrection. Chapter 2 thus contrasts the old in Judaism with the gospel of the new life which Jesus now offers to men.

But the Gospel writer does not tell the miracle story merely as a parable; he tells it as an event which actually occurred. The story had a symbolic meaning for him, but he was convinced that Jesus really turned the water into wine. We may have trouble accepting the miracle. Even though we concede that Jesus certainly did many remarkable deeds, we may still have questions about some of the stories. We must recognize, however, that in the view of the Gospel writer two things were basic: the gospel of new life came to men in an actual human life, and it was symbolized in actual marvelous deeds of Jesus. We may think that "miracles don't happen," but the Gospels present strong evidence that Jesus did many mighty deeds which indicated that God was uniquely present and active in him. If we have trouble accepting this story literally and think that possibly it grew in the telling, we should remember that the central figure of history may have done deeds which we and our Church today cannot match (but see 14:12!). At any rate, we should be clear about two points: Jesus did many remarkable acts, and they can be signs to us that God was powerfully present in him to give men life.

In the first three Gospels, Jesus centers his ministry in Galilee and especially at Capernaum. But this Gospel centers his ministry in Jerusalem, and mentions a stay in Capernaum only in 2:12.

Jesus stayed there only a "few days," and nothing he did there is reported. However, his mother and brothers as well as his disciples went with him from Cana to Capernaum. (Probably Joseph was now dead, but 6:42 does not indicate this.) The journey suggests either that Jesus moved his family home to Capernaum or that he and his family and disciples had been invited there. Verse 12 might seem to suggest that Jesus' family had become a permanent part of his traveling group, and in 19:25-27 his mother is said to have been present at the cross just outside Jerusalem; but only in 2:12 is it said that his family traveled with him, and in 7:5 his brothers' lack of faith in him indicates that his family did not actively support him during his ministry. (Mark 3:20-21, 31-35, points to the same conclusion.)

On the first visit which Jesus made to Jerusalem during his ministry he found the outer court of the Temple crowded and disturbed by noisy confusion (vs. 14). The main cause was the intrusion of business zeal. Some men were selling animals and birds for pilgrims to use in sacrifice. Also active were money-changers, who for a fee would supply pilgrims with the proper Jewish coins in exchange for foreign money, which was not acceptable for Temple gifts because it had the image of a Roman emperor and idolatrously suggested that he was divine. This Gospel does not suggest, as Matthew 21:13; Mark 11:17; and Luke 19:46 do, that the prices charged for sacrificial animals and for exchanging money were exorbitant and so were robbery of worshipers; nor does it suggest, as Mark 11:17 does, that such a commotion in the outer court of the Temple, the only part of the Temple area into which Gentiles could enter, made it impossible for Gentiles to worship. The one point here made is that to make this court a "house of trade" (vs. 16) cheapened it and kept people from thinking of it as "my Father's house," a place of reverent worship and grateful dedication. The Temple had become a commercial center rather than a place of worship.

Indignant at this profaning of the Temple, Jesus found some cords and made a whip (vs. 15). Did he use the whip on the money-minded traders or only on the animals he drove out of the Temple court? Probably the Greek means that he used it on both, to force the reluctant dealers as well as the animals to depart. In his burning wrath he also poured out the cash supply of the money-changers and overturned their tables, and urgently demanded that the sellers of pigeons take the birds away from the Temple (vs.

16). This Temple he called "my Father's house," and he would not let it be profaned. Nothing should be allowed to destroy the setting of worship, for which the Temple had been built. Jesus' burning determination to keep the Temple for its intended use recalled to the disciples the words of Psalm 69:9, "zeal for thy house will consume me" (vs. 17).

Up to this point the story seems to say simply that Jesus wanted to restore the Temple to its divinely intended use. But now an added point begins to emerge. The Jews asked him for a sign that would prove his right to act as he had done (vs. 18). He was not in charge of the Temple; the priests were. Unless he had authority from God to interfere with what the priests permitted, he was acting unlawfully.

As often in this Gospel, Jesus first makes an ambiguous statement; his hearers misunderstand it; and then it is explained (but this time only to the readers). His first saying was: "Destroy this temple, and in three days I will raise it up" (vs. 19). The Jews thought he was claiming that he could rebuild the Jerusalem Temple that quickly. They reminded him (vs. 20) that it had been under construction for forty-six years. (The main Temple building, which contained the Holy Place and Most Holy Place, had been rebuilt by Herod the Great in eighteen months, beginning in 20 or 19 B.C., but work on the other parts of the total Temple area had been going on during the rest of the forty-six years and was not yet ended; the entire group of buildings was not completed until about A.D. 64, shortly before the Romans destroyed the Temple in A.D. 70.) Since Herod the Great began rebuilding the Temple about 20-19 B.C., forty-six years would place this first Passover of Jesus' ministry about A.D. 26 or 27, which in this Gospel would suggest a date of about A.D. 29 or 30 for his death. But verse 21 says that the interest of Jesus was not in the Jerusalem Temple; he was speaking of the temple of his body (compare I Cor. 3:16; 6:19), and so was saying in veiled words that when they had put him to death, he would rise from the dead in three days, and would be the new and living center of men's worship.

Even his disciples, verse 22 indicates, did not understand his words at first; only after he had risen from the dead did they see what he must have meant. Then they realized that he knew in advance about his death and resurrection, "and they believed the scripture [that is, Ps. 69:9] and the word which Jesus had

spoken." They had already put their faith in him, but this new
insight gave an added basis for their faith, and the Gospel writer
brings out this point because his constant purpose was to deepen
and strengthen faith.

The Passover feast was celebrated at evening on the fourteenth
day of the month Nisan; it fell in March or April. The Feast of
Unleavened Bread followed, lasting seven days (Lev. 23:5-8).
The two feasts were so closely connected that either name might
be used for the entire period of the two feasts. Here the reference
to "the Passover feast" (vs. 23) probably includes the Feast of
Unleavened Bread. During that time Jesus presumably taught,
but what verse 23 particularly notes is that he performed deeds of
power which were signs that God was uniquely present and active in him. "Many believed in his name," that is, believed in him
in the light of what his works revealed of his divine power and
mission.

But the faith of these believers, founded mainly on miraculous
deeds, needed deepening in order to become full and firm faith.
So "Jesus did not trust himself to them"; he did not yet trust
their loyalty to prove steadfast (vs. 24). With his deep knowledge
of men and of the way they could fail to develop full and faithful
loyalty, he was not deceived into thinking that a faith based only
on outward deeds of power was adequate. Verses 24-25 reveal
something of his loneliness and of the patience with which he
had to wait for full and steady faith to develop. They show that
Jesus understood men; he was not deceived and surprised when
some followed him for a time and then drew back (6:66).

The Necessity for Spirit-Caused Rebirth (3:1-36)

In the Gospel of John the Pharisees are the prominent Jewish
leaders. Nicodemus, one of them, was "a ruler of the Jews" (vs.
1); that is, he was a member of the Sanhedrin, the highest Jewish court. The fact that he came "by night" to see Jesus (vs. 2),
and that in this Gospel darkness is the realm of evil, may suggest
that his motives were dark and ominous, or at least that essentially he still was tied to the evil world. But it may mean simply
that he was a sincere but cautious inquirer who did not want to
attract public attention. He called Jesus "Rabbi" (Teacher), a
term of respect used in addressing a Jewish teacher. He said
plainly that he and others considered Jesus "a teacher come from
God," though oddly enough what he mentioned to support this

judgment was not anything that Jesus had said in teaching but
rather the "signs," the remarkable deeds which to faith were
clues pointing to God's presence and working in Jesus. Nicodemus
was convinced that only by God's active power could Jesus do
such signs. When he said, "We know," he did not mean that all of
the Pharisees or Sanhedrin were convinced of Jesus' divine mission, but only that Nicodemus and some others, perhaps including a few Jewish leaders, had so decided (see 7:48; 12:42).

In reply Jesus did not direct attention to outward signs or truth-
ful teaching but to man's need of a rebirth effected by the Holy
Spirit (vs. 3). At first Jesus' meaning was not clear to Nicodemus.
The Greek word used is ambiguous; it can mean born "anew" or
born "from above." Nicodemus took Jesus to mean a second
physical birth (vs. 4). That would be impossible; how could he,
an old man, be born again as a baby? Then Jesus, following the
pattern often used in this Gospel, in which a first statement is
misunderstood and then explained, cleared up his meaning (vs.
5); he did not mean a second physical birth, but a new birth
brought about by God's Spirit, and so brought about from above,
by divine working. This rebirth comes by water and the Spirit,
that is, by baptism in which the really effective renewal of life
comes not from the water or the human minister but from the
working of the Holy Spirit. Only by that Spirit-caused renewal
can man enter the Kingdom of God. (Only here, in verses 3 and
5, does the Gospel of John refer to the Kingdom of God; but see
18:33-37. This Gospel usually describes the right new relation to
God as "eternal life.") A physical birth cannot give spiritual life
(vs. 6). Sinful man needs a spiritual renewal which only the divine power of the Holy Spirit can bring about. This is a mystery;
Jesus conceded that. The change is as mysterious and impossible
to see as is the wind which can be heard but not seen (vs. 8); but
the work of the Spirit, though invisible, is as real as is that of the
wind. (Both Greek and Aramaic have one word which can mean
either "wind" or "Spirit," so it is easy to see how Jesus came to use
this illustration.)

This necessity for a God-effected rebirth mystified Nicodemus;
he did not understand how it could occur (vs. 9). Jesus replied
that Nicodemus as a teacher in Israel should understand such
things (vs. 10). In the word "we" in verse 11 the Gospel writer
and the Church blend their voices with that of Jesus in a rebuke
of Nicodemus for hesitating to accept their witness to the gospel.

If Nicodemus has found it so hard to accept "earthly things"—
that is, this basic teaching about the necessity for a radical renewal as a condition for entering the Kingdom of God—how will
he be able to follow Jesus in further teaching about the full plan
of God? (vs. 12). The "heavenly things" seem to be the fuller
truth which Jesus could add about God's nature and plan and
his sending of his Son.

For what is our real touch with God and heavenly things?
Verses 13-15 say that it is the Son of Man, Jesus, who provides
constant communication between God and men (see 1:51). No
one has ascended into heaven to pierce the divine mysteries and
reveal the divine purpose except the One who descended from
heaven and "became flesh" (1:14); only Jesus, the crucified and
glorified Son of Man, provides the needed knowledge of God and
the needed redemptive working for man's salvation. An Old
Testament illustration helps to make this clear (vs. 14). In Numbers 21:9, after the Israelites had been bitten by poisonous ser-
pents, Moses at God's command set up a bronze serpent on a
pole. If anyone who was bitten looked at the bronze serpent, he
lived instead of dying from the poison. So the Son of Man had
to be lifted up on the cross in the midst of men poisoned by sin,
and whoever looks to him in faith will receive the divine gift of
eternal life (vs. 15).

Verses 16-21 explain further this gift of life through the death
of Jesus. The gift was given because of God's love for "the
world," that is, for all of sinful mankind. His love was so deep,
so determined to help sinful men, that he was even willing to give
his only Son to die on the cross to save them (vs. 16). Without
such adequate divine help, spiritual ruin and death loomed ahead
for all men. But whoever of any place or people believes in the
Son and gratefully accepts his saving work will receive eternal
life. The purpose of God in sending the Son was not to judge and
condemn mankind, but to save them through the work of the
Son (vs. 17). The believer is freed from the danger of condemnation (vs. 18); God's saving work in his Son has given him life
and placed him beyond the reach of the ruin and death that his
sin would otherwise bring. By his act of believing he has already
entered into true, full, and lasting life.

But whoever refuses to accept God's gift and believe in his
Son is condemned already. His condemnation does not wait until the final judgment; the act of rejecting the Son is the very time

of his judgment. He has had the opportunity to receive the gift of life, but he has rejected it and thereby has taken his stand outside of life and under condemnation.

Jesus describes the judgment by using the figure of light for God's presence and blessing, and the figure of darkness for God's absence and his condemnation of sin (vs. 19). The divine Word is "the light of men" and the incarnate Jesus is "the light of the world" (see 1:4; 8:12). This Light has come into the world to give men light and help, and yet sinful men, afraid to confess their sin honestly and ask divine forgiveness, have loved darkness, shunned the light, and tried vainly to hide their wickedness and need for salvation (vs. 20). They hate the light because it exposes their evil deeds. They fail to see that the divine light not only exposes and condemns man's evil way of living but also brings divine forgiveness, cleansing, and power; and so it takes away sin and guilt and gives a new birth and a new power to love and obey God. They further fail to see that once forgiven and reborn, man can live in the light without shame and condemnation. This is not his own achievement; it is rather the gracious work of God. As a reborn child of God he can now accept and do God's will, and in that new life the light does not shame and condemn; it discloses that the believer's deeds have been done by God's power and according to God's will (vs. 21).

Jesus had been in Jerusalem (2:13, 23); it was there that Nicodemus talked to him (3:1-2). He next went with his disciples to some unnamed place in Judea and there, for an undefined time, he preached and baptized those who believed in response to his preaching (vs. 22). That Jesus baptized is stated in verses 22, 26, repeated in 4:1, and then corrected in 4:2; his disciples actually did the baptizing. John the Baptist had not yet been imprisoned (vs. 24); he was still preaching and baptizing, but no longer at Bethany beyond the Jordan (1:28); he had moved to Aenon near Salim, where much water provided a good place for a kind of baptism that seems to have involved the candidate's immersion of himself, at John's command, in the water in which he stood (vs. 23). John preached at Aenon and baptized those who accepted his preaching.

Followers of John had a dispute with a Jew about purifying (vs. 25). The question perhaps was how men are really purified. From the standpoint of this Gospel, only the Lamb of God, by taking away the sin of the world (1:29), and the Spirit, by bring-

ing about a rebirth at baptism (3:5), can really purify a life de-
filed by sin. John had not claimed to give the full blessing of
purification and life, but only to prepare for him who could give
it. Had John's disciples claimed more for his baptism than John
himself had? In any case, the role of Jesus was brought up, for
John's disciples reported to him that Jesus, to whom John had
earlier given his witness (1:29-36), was baptizing and winning
universal acceptance (3:26). The statement that "all" were going
to Jesus is an exaggerated way of saying that great throngs, larger
than those coming to John, were going to hear Jesus and to be
baptized by him.

John renewed his witness to Jesus; for the Gospel writer this
refuted his contemporaries who still followed John rather than
Jesus. Each man, John said, must accept and fulfill the role given
him by heaven, that is, by God (vs. 27). John had not claimed to
be the Christ but only to be sent before him to prepare for his
coming (vs. 28; by this statement the Gospel writer implies that
John now held Jesus to be the Christ). To illustrate his own preparatory and lesser role, John likened himself to the friend of the
bridegroom, who arranges for the marriage and makes all the
plans (vs. 29). When the bridegroom and bride come to their new
home, the friend has finished his duties, and rejoices at the bridegroom's happiness. So John had called Israel to believe in Jesus,
and now that this great response showed that Israel was going to
Jesus as John wanted them to do, he as the friend of Jesus could
count his work done and rejoice in the success of Jesus' ministry.
The plan of God ("must" in vs. 30 refers to the divine plan and
necessity) is that Jesus must increase, that is, have increasing
success and importance, while John decreases, that is, plays an
ever decreasing role in the development of God's purpose. Israel
must center its attention on Jesus rather than on John; "the
Church's one Foundation is Jesus Christ her Lord." He who had
come onto the scene of historical action and public ministry after
John had begun his work had now come to take a rank before
John (1:15, 30).

This Gospel more than once starts to report (with interpretation) a historical incident, but soon drops all reference to that
incident and speaks in general terms of what Jesus' coming means.
So in the beginning of chapter 3 Nicodemus talks with Jesus, but
by the time we come to 3:16-21 what we hear is not a dialogue
with Nicodemus, but the evangelist's explanation of how God has

provided eternal life for men through his Son. Likewise in 3:31-36 the words of the Baptist have given way completely to the evangelist's statement of Christ's origin, witness, and work.

Christ came from above, sent by the Father (vs. 31). As the Son he ranks above John and all other human leaders. An earthly leader can only tell of things he knows. Even a man used by God cannot reveal God's nature and purpose in any full and final way; his vision and understanding do not reach that far. Only the Son can fully reveal God and effectively provide salvation. He, the Son, testifies to what he knows of the Father and can reveal the full sweep of the Father's work and purpose (vs. 32). Even so, he finds no acceptance, that is, no general acceptance; the sweeping statement that "all" were receiving him (vs. 26) is here corrected in view of the final rejection of Jesus by most of his hearers. But those who, like the Gospel writer, receive Jesus' testimony in faith know it is true and testify that God is true to himself and that his Son is true to him (vs. 33). The Son whom God has sent speaks just what the Father sent him to say, for the Father gave the Son the Spirit in full measure (vs. 34), and in love for the Son entrusted to him the carrying out of the entire divine plan (vs. 35). So man's relation to God is determined by his relation to the Son; faith in the Son is the divinely established way to receive God's grace and gifts and power.

Therefore verse 36 is as basic as the famous 3:16. Everyone who believes in the Son as sent of God to take away man's sin and to give life to those dead in sin receives at once eternal life. Eternal life is a relation of unmarred fellowship with the Father and the Son (17:3); it opens to the believer every blessing and privilege that makes for spiritual health and growth. But whoever refuses the gospel message and will not believe in and obey the Son will not see that eternal life. The wrath of God, the divine judgment, immediately and relentlessly rests on the unrepentant sinner who stubbornly rejects the offer of grace and life. There is no place for neutrality. Man was made as a moral being who can really live only by being obedient to his Father. He must either believe, obey God, and find eternal life, or refuse and so suffer the ruin that his evil choice makes inevitable.

Jesus the Savior of the World (4:1-54)

Jesus left Judea for Galilee after a remarkably successful ministry in Judea (3:26). (The other Gospels do not mention a Ju-

dean ministry until the last week of Jesus' life.) Success had
stirred up hostility. The Pharisees, regarded as the chief leaders of
the Jews, realized that the response to Jesus was even greater than
that which John the Baptist had received; Jesus was baptizing
more disciples than John (vs. 1; compare 3:22). Here again this
Gospel, having first made an unqualified statement, qualifies it:
Jesus himself did not baptize at all; he left that to his disciples
(vs. 2; see I Cor. 1:13-17). The only references in the four Gospels to baptism by Jesus are 3:22, 26 and 4:1-2; if he baptized
at all, he obviously did not emphasize baptism in the way John
did. But if he did direct or approve baptism by his disciples, it
would help us understand how according to Acts the Church
baptized converts from the very beginning (Acts 2:38, 41). At
any rate, John 4:1 indicates that official opposition led Jesus to
break off his successful ministry in Judea and travel north to Galilee (vs. 3).

Jesus could have gone east from Judea (3:22), crossed the Jordan River, traveled north, and then recrossed the river to enter
Galilee just below the Sea of Galilee. Galilean pilgrims often took
that route to and from Jerusalem, to avoid contact with the hated
Samaritans. But when they wanted to save time they took the
direct route north from Judea through Samaria. This is what
Jesus did; a divine purpose made this necessary (vs. 4). He came
to Sychar (vs. 5), a Samaritan city close to Jacob's Well, at noon
(the sixth hour), the hot time of the day. Tired from walking,
Jesus sat by the well while the disciples went into Sychar to buy
food (vss. 6, 8). Sychar probably was either a now vanished village at the foot of Mount Gerizim or the city of Shechem, a little
to the west of Jacob's Well.

Carrying water was woman's work. When a Samaritan woman
came to Jacob's Well to draw water, Jesus, hot and thirsty, asked
her for a drink (vs. 7). He had no bucket with which to draw
water for himself (vs. 11). The request surprised her for two
reasons: it was not usual for a man to talk to a strange woman,
and it was especially unusual for a Jew to ask a favor of a
Samaritan woman, because Jews dealt with Samaritans as little
as possible (vs. 9).

Jesus turned the conversation to the gift of living water that he
could give her (vs. 10). "Living water" could mean flowing fresh
water, but he meant life-giving water, water that could give eternal
life (this was close to saying, "I am the water of life"; compare

6:35—"I am the bread of life"). If the woman had known what God was ready to give, and who it was that was asking her for a drink, she would have realized that he had more to give to her than she could give to him, and would have asked him for the living water which he could give her. But she still thought only of water from Jacob's Well. Jesus had no bucket with which to draw water from the deep well, yet he claimed to have fresh water. This puzzled her. She vaguely sensed that he claimed to have a source other than this well, which had provided water for Jacob (whom she claimed as the ancestor of the Samaritans: "our father") and for his family and livestock. She challenged his claim (vs. 12). Jacob had to get his water from this well; was Jesus greater than Jacob? She had no comprehension of how much greater Jesus was.

Jesus turned the woman's attention away from this well water. It could only temporarily satisfy men's physical thirst (vs. 13). Jesus can give a different water which will permanently satisfy men's thirst; it will become a spring of ever-flowing blessing which will give eternal life to the one who drinks it (vs. 14). He referred to the life-giving divine blessing which faith would enable the believer to receive. But the woman, still thinking of well water and the daily trip she had to make to the well, asked for this water which Jesus meant, so that she would never again thirst and have to come to the well and draw water (vs. 15).

Jesus got at her spiritual and moral problem by asking her to go and call her husband (vs. 16). When she denied having a husband (vs. 17), Jesus showed that though he had not seen her before, he knew her actual life situation. She had had five husbands and was now living with still another man, who was not her lawful husband (vs. 18). It is hardly likely that so many husbands had all died a natural death, each leaving her a widow free to remarry. Probably she had gone by divorce from one unhappy marriage to another, and was now living with a man without a lawful marriage. It has been suggested that by the five husbands Jesus meant the five gods of the five places from which the king of Assyria brought settlers to Samaria to replace the Israelite people deported from Samaria (II Kings 17:24), and that the woman's illegal partner was the Samaritan religion, an unlawful form of the faith of Israel. But II Kings 17:24 does not say that each of the five cities named had only one god. Jesus probably was speaking simply of the woman's marital laxity.

Either from embarrassment at the exposure of her lax life, or from idle curiosity, the woman turned the discussion to theological matters. In Jesus' ability to discern her life situation she saw evidence that he was a prophet (vs. 19), so she tried to turn attention away from her personal sin to a more comfortable general subject. Her ancestors had worshiped on Mount Gerizim, at the foot of which they were standing, and she expected Jesus as a Jew to defend the Jewish claim that the worship of the Father must take place at the Temple in Jerusalem (vs. 20). But instead he announced the end of the days when worship was tied to a particular place (vs. 21).

Jesus did not disown his Jewish heritage. The Jews had been the real Covenant People; their worship had been the divinely authorized worship at the divinely chosen place in Jerusalem; the saving plan of God had been carried along by God's dealings with the (often rebellious) Jews, so that salvation, while entirely due to God's grace and not to Jewish goodness or greatness, comes to mankind from and through the Jews (vs. 22). But the time had come when neither Mount Gerizim nor the Temple in Jerusalem could claim to be the place where men must center their worship.

God the Father is not a physical being limited to one place; as Spirit he is present in all places, and true spiritual worship may be given to him in any place (vss. 23-24). He had now brought mankind to the time in his redemptive plan when all limitations of place were to fall away and men could give him spiritual worship in any and every place—in the home or shop or field as truly as in the Temple or synagogue, in Syria or Greece or Egypt as truly as in Jerusalem or on Mount Gerizim. Henceforth special places of worship had no right to exist except to help worshipers realize this universal presence of God. Jesus declared it to be thoroughly wrong to think that one place or building is sacred while other places or buildings are without God's presence.

Jesus thus indicated that in his work God's final purpose was being realized. But most Samaritans and Jews expected the coming of the Messiah (or Christ; both words mean "anointed" and refer to God's great final leader). He would come to complete God's plan and teach God's full will. The woman was ready to postpone such questions as the final form of true worship until the Messiah should come and lead his people to the perfect expression of loyalty to God (vs. 25). Jesus frankly and clearly told her that he was that expected Messiah—for Samaritans as well as for Jews, and so for all men (vs. 26). He had come with the mission and authority to lead people to the knowledge and worship which would establish God's intended order among all his people. This claim Andrew had discerned (1:41); it is expressed or implied in all the great titles given to Jesus throughout this Gospel; the Gospel was written to urge the claim upon its readers (20:31).

When the disciples returned from Sychar, presumably with the food they had gone to buy (vs. 8), the woman, too excited and in too great a hurry to remember her water jar, hastened away to the city to tell people of this remarkable teacher (vss. 27-29). The disciples, like the woman (vs. 9), were surprised that Jesus was talking with a Samaritan woman, but they knew that his ministry often broke away from usual Jewish custom, so they did not question or criticize him. The woman's report to the men of Sychar mentioned two things: (1) Jesus had shown astounding ability to lay bare her past. With extravagant exaggeration she said that he had told her everything she had ever done. (2) He might even be the expected Christ. She did not report as fact what he had so plainly stated (vs. 26); she only suggested it cautiously as a live possibility. Verses 39 and 42 may imply that she really accepted his claim. In any case, her report stirred the men of the city; they started for Jacob's Well to see this notable visitor (vs. 30).

In the meantime Jesus, talking with his disciples, brought out his urgent concern for the great task that confronted him and them. When they offered him the food they had bought (vs. 31), he said that he had other food unknown to them (vs. 32). They, as so often happens in this Gospel, misunderstood him; they thought someone else must have given him ordinary food while they were in the city (vs. 33). So Jesus told them what his real food was (vs. 34). The food for which he hungered was to do the will of the Father who had sent him and thus complete the work the Father had sent him to do (compare Matt. 5:6).

Then Jesus saw the people of Sychar streaming along the road from the city to Jacob's Well, and he used the situation as a parable of the urgency of the work which he was doing and the disciples were to do. There was a proverb that four months after planting the seed, the harvest would come (vs. 35). But right after his talk with the Samaritan woman and her quick report in the city, the men of the city were hurrying to see and hear him. The harvest was following the sowing without a four-month wait. The fields were white for harvest; the Samaritans were ready to accept the gospel without delay. The disciples could step in, lead these people to faith, and so gain the lasting spiritual reward which awaited faithful workers for God's Christ (vs. 36). But the fact that the disciples could step in and by leading the Samaritans to faith could reap the harvest for which Jesus and the Samaritan woman had sown the seed should remind them that the harvester does not deserve all the credit (vss. 37-38). Just as it is God who puts life into the grain seed, so here Jesus, and to a lesser degree the Samaritan woman, had sown the seed. But the speed with which harvest followed sowing should make the disciples realize how urgent the task was and how great the possibility of a quickly fruitful ministry would always be. (At this point the Gospel writer is thinking much more of the later work of the disciples than of their work at Sychar.)

The response of the people of Sychar was a symbol of the world-wide response to Christ in a new worship in spirit and truth (vs. 23). It illustrated again this Gospel's point that men must go on from an initial faith to a deeper and fuller faith. Many believed in Jesus because of the woman's testimony to Jesus (vs. 39); the fact that he could tell her all that she had done convinced them that he was a God-sent leader, so they went to him and asked him to stay with them (vs. 40). During his two-day visit, the initial faith grew in two ways: more people believed in him on the basis of his own teaching (vs. 41), and all who believed, it is implied, had now a more solid ground for their faith than the woman's report (vs. 42). They had heard for themselves; they had faced Jesus and his claim; they had come to know with certainty that he was the Savior of the world. The true worship of God was no longer confined to or centered in Jerusalem; it was open to all who would believe that Jesus is the Christ, the Son of God (20:31). The Christ had come not for the Jews alone, nor even for Jews and Samaritans alone, but for the world. If the official who asked for help in 4:46-47 was a Gentile, this was still further stress upon the universal outreach of the gospel.

After the fruitful two-day visit in Sychar, Jesus continued his journey to Galilee (vs. 43). He was welcomed there (vs. 45) because of the remarkable ministry he had carried on in Jeru-

salem, especially at the feast (apparently the Passover of 2:13).
Numerous Galileans had gone to that feast, had seen what Jesus
did, and so had reason to welcome him when he returned to Galilee. Verse 44, that "a prophet has no honor in his own country,"
is puzzling. In Matthew 13:57; Mark 6:4; and Luke 4:24, essentially the same saying refers to Nazareth as Jesus' native place
which was unwilling to accept his claims. Here "his own country"
may possibly refer to Galilee generally, and may mean that although usually a prophet is not accepted in his native place,
Jesus as a Galilean was nevertheless welcomed back to Galilee
because of his remarkable deeds in Jerusalem. But more likely
verse 44 means that Judea was Jesus' true home and central place
of ministry, and that while Jesus received no real and trustworthy
welcome in Judea, where opposition to him centered (yet see
4:1-3), he was welcomed when he withdrew temporarily to
Galilee.

Only one incident of this Galilean visit is reported (vss. 46-
54). Jesus revisited Cana, where he had done his first sign (2:1-
11). While he was there, the son of an official who served Herod
Antipas, tetrarch of Galilee and Perea (4 B.C.—A.D. 39), was ill
and about to die (vss. 46-47). Apparently physicians could give
no help. This official, who lived at Capernaum, may have been a
Gentile; the centurion in the similar story in Matthew 8:5-13
and Luke 7:2-10 was probably not a Jew, and here Jesus, instead
of going to the official's home, healed at a distance, a method
used elsewhere in the Gospels only in dealing with Gentiles.

This official knew of Jesus' power to heal, heard of his return
to Galilee, and hurried to Cana to ask him to come to Capernaum and heal his son. Jesus tested his faith by suggesting that
he would not believe in Jesus without seeing signs and wonders
(vs. 48). The man could not wait to discuss reasons for believing; in anguish and haste—and with some real faith—he repeated his appeal for Jesus to come before it was too late to save
his son's life (vs. 49). Jesus told him to go home and promised
that his son would live (vs. 50); he thus asked the father to believe in him without seeing any outward sign, such as Jesus'
willingness to go with him to help his son.

The man believed that Jesus had the power to help, that the
promise was good, and that the son would live. In that faith he
started back to Capernaum. On the way his servants met him and
reported gladly that his son was alive and recovering (vs. 51).

The son took the turn for the better, they said, at the seventh hour (probably 1:00 p.m., though some would take this to mean 7:00 p.m.), and that was exactly when Jesus had told the father that his son would live (vss. 52-53). The father had shown faith in accepting the promise of Jesus and returning home; now he "believed" in a deeper sense, and his entire household joined with him in believing in Jesus as sent of God and worthy of their faith. If, as seems probable, the father and his household were Gentiles, this points up again the full meaning of Jesus' ministry; he is "the Savior" not simply of Jews but "of the world" (vs. 42).

This healing is called "the second sign" done in Galilee (vs. 54); the first was told in 2:1-11. "Sign" means a remarkable deed of Jesus in which the eye of faith sees God present and uniquely active in Jesus to waken men to faith and so give them eternal life.

Jesus' Ministry Met by Both Faith and Unbelief (5:1—12:50)

Jesus Persecuted for Healing a Sick Man (5:1-47)

After the brief account of Jesus' stay in Galilee (4:43-54), where the only ministry reported consisted of one healing, the Gospel returns to Jerusalem. Jesus went for "a feast"; some ancient manuscripts say "the feast," which could mean the Feast of Tabernacles in the fall (Lev. 23:33-34), but the better evidence says "a feast." If chapter 6 were placed, as some suggest, before chapter 5, the reference in 5:1 might then be to the Passover, referred to as near in 6:4. The vague reference to "a feast," however, does not favor this; we cannot say which feast it was. But the reference to a feast reminds us that in this Gospel, Jesus appeared in Jerusalem at a series of feasts, to join in their celebration and to teach the large crowds which attended them.

North of the Temple, in the eastern part of the city, was the Sheep Gate (Neh. 3:1; 12:39). Near it was a pool surrounded by five porticoes or cloisters (vs. 2); a double pool discovered a few decades ago north of the Temple area probably was the scene of this story. The pool's name is given in Aramaic (which is what "in Hebrew" can mean, and here must mean, because the name given is Aramaic). The name probably was "Bethzatha," as some ancient Greek manuscripts read. But other manuscripts read instead either "Bethesda" or "Belzetha" or "Bethsaida"; the ancient Greek scribes evidently were puzzled by this foreign word.

The pool, it seems, was fed by an intermittent spring, which from time to time gushed forth water into the pool and so caused movement in the water; verse 7 refers to this, and so do verses 3b-4, but the words of verses 3b-4 are probably a later scribe's addition, since important early manuscripts omit them. The mysterious movement of the water was thought to bring healing to the first sick person who stepped into the water after the movement began. Many sick people, suffering from various ailments, were by the pool (vs. 3). Each hoped to be the first to get into the pool the next time the water was disturbed. There was even one man, sick for thirty-eight years, who had no one to put him into the water, but who apparently hoped that some kind stranger would help him (vs. 5). The kind stranger came; it was Jesus. He sensed the man's hopeless condition and asked him if he wanted to be healed (vs. 6). The sick man could not move fast enough to be the first to get into the pool, and since he had no one to help him, he saw no hope of healing (vs. 7). Jesus told him to rise from his pallet, pick it up with his newly given strength, and walk as a healthy man (vs. 8). The man responded in faith, was healed at once, and walked homeward carrying his pallet (vs. 9).

Controversy arose because the healing occurred on a Sabbath (vs. 9), when the Mosaic law prohibited work (Exod. 20:10). Since carrying the pallet was considered work, the man was rebuked by the Jews, who wanted all Sabbath rules faithfully kept (vs. 10). The man's defense was that the one who healed him had told him to pick up his pallet and walk (vs. 11). This shifted at least some of the blame to the healer, so the defenders of the Sabbath asked who the healer was (vs. 12). The man did not know Jesus' name; Jesus had left him and mingled with the crowd that thronged the place (vs. 13). Later Jesus found the man again. He was interested in the man's spiritual life even more than in his physical health, so he warned him to sin no more lest something worse than his previous illness should happen to him (vs. 14). This suggests that his previous illness had been due to his sinful life, and that further sin might cause even worse physical illness, although in 9:3, as in Luke 13:1-5, Jesus denies that sin and physical suffering are invariably connected. Sin often brings physical suffering, but the inevitable bad effects of sin are not always physical.

Nothing is said of the man's later faith or loyalty to Jesus. We are only told that when he learned the name of Jesus, he told his critics who had healed him (vs. 15). The result was that the Jews transferred their attack to Jesus for causing the man to do work on the Sabbath and so to break the Law (vs. 16). They did not rejoice that God's power had healed one of their suffering people; they did not see that such a gift of health and new life warranted the simple act of carrying home the pallet; they thought only of the necessity for a Jew to do nothing on the Sabbath that could be called work. Jesus replied that his Father, God, works constantly (vs. 17). To keep men alive and maintain the order of nature, God is active seven days a week and in that respect does not keep the Sabbath. So Jesus insisted that he, like his Father, must do good and meet human need on the Sabbath as well as on other days. Human suffering had a claim on him whenever he met it; he healed, not because he had scorn for the Sabbath day of rest, but because human need took precedence over the usual rule of rest.

In this reply the critics saw an even worse sin than breaking the Sabbath. Jesus, they sensed, was claiming a close and unique tie with the Father: he was calling God his Father in a sense that other men could not use; he was claiming divine nature and authority, and therefore equality with the Father. They took it for granted that this claim was false. Verse 18 implies that they had already been plotting to kill Jesus and that his claim made them even more determined to do so. But the power and helpfulness shown in the healing should have suggested to them another explanation, that Jesus' act was due to the active presence of God in him. In their blind zeal for their Law they failed to follow up this clue to who Jesus was and what he could do for them.

In verses 19-30 the full scope of Jesus' work is explored. Jesus speaks as the Son of God, conscious that he can do nothing except by faithfully doing what the Father does and wants him to do. He sees the ways of the Father, and follows them in every situation (vs. 19). The Father loves him, shows him all that he does, and will show him still greater works to do (vs. 20). This greater working is the giving of life. It is described as raising the dead (vs. 21), and as verse 24 shows, this means not merely raising those who are physically dead (as Lazarus was in chapter 11), but giving life to those who, though physically alive, are spiritually dead. By faith they may even now receive the gift of eternal life.

But the Son is sent not only to give life, but also to carry out for the Father the divine judgment (vs. 22). On the other occasions, to make clear that the basic reason for his coming was to save men, Jesus denies that he came to judge (3:17; 12:47). Yet his coming and the offer of eternal life through faith inevitably bring a judgment on all who refuse the divine offer. The divine purpose of the Father, in thus sending his Son to give life and to judge, is in part that men may honor the Son as surely and as much as they honor the Father (vs. 23). To fail to receive and honor and follow the Son is to dishonor and reject the Father who sent him. For the Father sent the Son; the divinely appointed way of salvation is to hear the Son and believe in him; to believe brings the immediate gift of eternal life (vs. 24).

Verses 25-29 picture two resurrections, two stages in the gift of life. In a real sense the sinner who hears Jesus' word and believes in him has eternal life immediately (3:36; 5:24). The hour of salvation has come for that man; he passes from spiritual death into spiritual life when he responds to the voice of the Son of God calling him to hear and believe (vs. 25). Just as the Father is the living and life-giving God, so the Son has life in himself (vs. 26). "In him was life, and the life was the light of men" (1:4), and in the gospel he offers that life to men. Only if men reject that divine offer of life does judgment occur, but then it surely and promptly will occur, because the Son has full authority from the Father to execute judgment on those who reject the offered gift of life (vs. 27). As the Son of Man, the divine Mediator between the Father and men (1:51), Jesus has authority both to save those who believe and to condemn those who refuse to turn from disobedience to faith.

No man is out of reach of Jesus' power to judge. Not even the dead are beyond his reach (vs. 28). The resurrection will come; at the voice of the Son all the dead will be raised. As the divine Judge, Jesus will assign the eternal lot of each one: those who have done good, who have believed in Jesus and obeyed his word, will be raised to enjoy forever the eternal life which they had already begun to enjoy from the time of the clear decision to believe in him; those who have done evil, who have rejected his claim and lived contrary to the divine demand, will be raised to receive the final and irrevocable sentence of condemnation (vs. 29). The Gospel writer no doubt thinks that the Son will judge all men of all generations, but in the words about judging those who have "done good" and those who have "done evil" the main reference is to those who have accepted or rejected the claim of Jesus.

But Jesus will not judge on his own authority. As verse 19 has said, he does not act independently, but only in obedience to the Father; the Father's will is always normative for him, and so in his judging, as in all his ministry, he carries out the divine will (vs. 30).

The remainder of chapter 5 presents witnesses to the divine mission of Jesus. Verse 31 recognizes that Jesus' claim would not be accepted simply on his own assertion (although in 8:13-18 he says that since what he says is true and is supported by the Father, his own statements do constitute one witness that God has sent him). He names five witnesses that attest his divine mission and his right to claim men's faith:

1. The Father. The witness in verse 32 might seem to be John the Baptist, since John is obviously the witness named in verse 33. But verse 32 connects with the reference to the Father at the end of verse 30. So the first testimony to Jesus here cited is that of the Father, and it is repeated in verse 37.

2. John the Baptist. Already in 1:6-8, 15, 19-36, and 3:25-30 the witness of John has been reported; it obviously was important to the Gospel writer, who possibly had once been a disciple of John before believing in Jesus. The Jews had sent to John (1:19) and received John's witness to Jesus (5:33). Jesus knows that human witness is not the final basis of his authority and vindication; that can come only from the Father. But the human witness may help others to believe, and so it serves a necessary and saving function, which Jesus does not despise (vs. 34). John as a shining lamp was a witness to Jesus the Light of the world; John's hearers had regarded him as divinely sent to give light to God's people (vs. 35), and they should now let the light of John's witness guide them to believe in the true Light.

3. The works of Jesus. Even more important to Jesus than the witness of John were the deeds which Jesus himself did by the Father's power and authority (vs. 36). Whoever will open his eyes to the divine power and beneficent effects of these deeds will see

God at work in Jesus and so will be led to believe in him. That faith is the intended result of the witness which the works bear to Jesus. The witness of the Father is the basic and finally authoritative witness. Already mentioned in verse 32, it is repeated in verses 37-38. As 1:18 said, "No one has ever seen God"; Jesus' hearers have not heard God speaking directly to man. God has acted by sending his Son, and he who has seen and known the Son has seen the Father (14:8-11). The Father's word has no hold on the hearers or they would believe in Jesus, and their earlier and continuing opportunity to hear that word—through the Scriptures—is now stated clearly.

4. The Scriptures. Rightly understood, the Old Testament is a witness to Jesus. (That is why the Old Testament was kept as a part of Christian Scripture; otherwise, it should be discarded by the Church.) Verse 39 probably begins not with a command, "Search the scriptures," though the Greek could be so translated, but with a statement of fact: "You [Jews] search the scriptures," but miss their deepest truth, for these writings witness to Jesus, and by missing that point and refusing to believe in Jesus the searchers miss the eternal life that the Scriptures promise and Jesus came to give (vs. 40). Jesus says this not because he wants men's praise and honor (vs. 41), but to rebuke the lack of love for God in his hearers (vs. 42). If they had that love, they would respond to the witness which Scripture and the Father give to Jesus; as it is, they are so misguided that they reject the One sent by the Father, and they seem ready to accept any other leader who comes without being sent by God (vs. 43). The honor that God gives is all that counts; the competitive struggle among his hearers for human honor and praise keeps them from valuing the witness and praise of God and so keeps them from believing in the Son whom God has sent to them (vs. 44).

5. Moses. The witness of Moses (vs. 46) is essentially identical with the already mentioned witness of the Scriptures. But there is point in singling out Moses for special mention, for the Jews credited Moses with giving them the Law, and they took the Law as their basis for condemning Jesus. In reality, Moses, rightly understood, wrote of Jesus. (The writer cites no specific passages. Did he think of such verses as Genesis 49:10 and Deuteronomy 18:15, 18?) If they really understood Moses and his testimony to the One who was to come, they would believe in Jesus and receive the gift of life. But as it is, they reject the deepest meaning

of Moses' message to God's people, and so they refuse to believe
what Jesus says (vs. 47). The Moses they try to use to oppose
Jesus really condemns them for not believing in Jesus (vs. 45).

Jesus the Bread of Life Rejected by Many (6:1-71)

In 6:1 Jesus seems to start from the west side of the Sea of
Galilee and cross to the east or northeast shore (see vss. 16-17,
24-25). But in chapter 5 Jesus has been in Jerusalem (5:1-2). It
is often suggested that originally chapter 6 followed chapter 4,
which ends with Jesus in Galilee; then Jesus, in Galilee in 4:46,
could go to the Sea of Galilee and cross it as 6:1 says he did. But
if chapter 6 originally preceded chapter 5, it is hard to say how or
why that order was changed, so we may hold that the Gospel
writer put the material in the order we now have. He apparently
wrote separate sections without much concern to knit them closely
together.

The need of food for five thousand men arose shortly after
Jesus crossed the Sea of Galilee. This lake was sometimes called
the Sea of Tiberias, particularly from the late first century on; it
was named thus after the city of Tiberias, built by Herod the
Great about A.D. 22 on the west shore of that lake. Jesus sailed
perhaps from Capernaum, on the northwest shore of the lake, the
city at which he landed on his return voyage (vss. 24-25). The
crowd, interested by the signs of healing he had done, followed
on land (vs. 2), crossing the Jordan just where it entered the lake,
and continuing east to where Jesus had landed, in a region where
hills rose near the shore (vs. 3; this could be near the northeast
shore). His disciples were with him.

It was Passover time (vs. 4), late March or early April; this is
the one Jewish feast mentioned in this Gospel for which Jesus did
not go to Jerusalem. It is mentioned here because Jesus would die
in Jerusalem at the next Passover (11:55), and would be "the
Lamb of God, who takes away the sin of the world" (1:29); the
miracle at the Passover season in chapter 6 interpreted not only
the meaning of Jesus' life but especially and in advance the meaning of his death. The crowd which Jesus saw approaching were
not, as often thought, on their way southward from northern regions to Jerusalem to celebrate the Passover there. The people
were not on a main highway to Jerusalem; they were coming east-
ward, as verses 2 and 5 show, because of their interest in Jesus.

Jesus took the initiative in feeding this multitude. To test Philip,

Jesus asked how they could get bread to feed so many (vs. 5; the number 5,000 is given in vs. 10). But Jesus already had his plan formed (vs. 6). Philip had no answer; he thought only of the usual method, buying bread, but the cost appalled him (vs. 7)—two hundred denarii would not buy enough to give a small portion to each person. (A denarius, about twenty cents in value, was about a day's wage for common labor.) Andrew had an equally inadequate suggestion (vss. 8-9); he had seen a boy with five barley loaves (barley bread was cheaper than wheat bread) and two fish, but he knew that this would not meet the need. The two disciples thus made it clear that human resources and planning could not satisfy the multitude.

Jesus had the disciples make the crowd sit down on the spring grass (vs. 10). Then he took the boy's five barley loaves, gave thanks, and (evidently through the disciples) distributed them to all; he did the same with the fish (vs. 11). The miracle is not described or explained, but it is implied that the amount of bread and fish was immensely increased, so that all could eat their fill (vs. 12). That twelve baskets of fragments of bread were left over showed how generously Jesus had provided for the needs of all present (vs. 13).

The writer clearly sees in this story a symbol of Jesus as the Bread of Life (6:35), who feeds his people with every spiritual gift they need for full and good life. But the writer was equally convinced that this increase of the supply of bread and fish actually happened; it was a real event and also a symbol of vital spiritual truth. We cannot explain such a story. We may debate whether it grew from a parable, or from a much more modest act of Jesus, or whether the powerful presence of God in the incarnate Word made possible and fitting so remarkable an act of divine power; but the clear intent of the writer was to report an actual miracle and then show what it should teach the believer. The modern believer may consider it possible that the story has grown in the telling, but he will not try to limit the action of Jesus to what good men can commonly do.

The effect of the miracle on the crowd was striking (vs. 15). Often in this Gospel the crowd divides in its view of Jesus; here they all saw God at work in Jesus, and decided that he must be the prophet like Moses, promised to God's people in Deuteronomy 18:15, 18. It may seem strange to us that they would want to make a prophet their king, but Jewish expectations that God

would send a great leader at the climax of their history combined
several Old Testament ideas of leadership, including the prophet
and the Davidic king. It was expected that the great final leader
of God's people would feed them, as Moses fed Israel in the
wilderness (Exodus 16), so this miracle could suggest that the
great leader had come and was about to establish God's Kingdom.
But the political goals implicit in the popular idea of a Davidic
king Jesus could not accept, so he withdrew to a lonely place,
higher in the hills than the place where he had met the crowd
(vss. 3, 15).

Another remarkable experience followed. It affected only the
disciples who, when evening came, left the crowd, went down to
the shore, got into their boat, and started westward to Capernaum
(vss. 16-17). They had hoped or expected that Jesus would go
with them, but he did not come, so they went ahead without him.
The wind was against them, so they could not use a sail; they had
to row and the wind made this hard because of the waves it raised
(vs. 18). After a hard row had taken them three or four miles
(twenty-five or thirty stadia; a stade was 600 feet), they saw
Jesus approaching, walking on the rough water (vs. 19). They
were frightened, not for fear that he might sink and drown, but
because this act of his suggested a mysterious divine power which
they did not understand. Perhaps verse 20 suggests also that they
were not really sure that it was Jesus, and feared it might be some
hostile spirit. But at his reassuring word their fear vanished, they
were glad to receive him into the boat, and they at once reached
the land, which, as verses 24-25 show, was the shore at Capernaum.

Some infer from verse 21 that Jesus was not really walking on
deep water, but was in shallow water near the shore, as the disciples realized when their fear left them. But the writer seems to
mean that by his unique power Jesus had walked on deep water,
and that the voyage went easily and swiftly once the disciples
recognized that Jesus was with them in the storm. To the writer
this undoubtedly taught the disciples to trust in Jesus in the
stormy times of their life and service.

The crowd spent the night on the east or northeast shore of the
lake. They evidently did not see Jesus leave that region to meet
the disciples (vs. 22). But they saw the disciples leave, and they
finally concluded that Jesus had followed his disciples in some un-
noticed way. They boarded boats from Tiberias which came near

the shore where they were. These were probably fishing boats. By some means the crowd got the shipowners and sailors to take them to Capernaum, a known center of Jesus' ministry (vss. 23-24).

There they found him (vs. 25). Their first question was superficial. Calling him "Rabbi" (Teacher), they asked when he came there. His reply went directly to the reason they were hunting for him (vs. 26). It was not because they saw in the feeding of the five thousand (and in other similar miracles) signs of God's presence and power at work in him, and so were led to believe in him, but because their physical hunger was satisfied. They thought of him merely as a provider for physical needs. Instead of seeking food to satisfy physical hunger, they should look to him for the spiritual food that sustains eternal life (vs. 27). This food the Son of Man (Jesus) could give, for the Father had approved his ministry. (In the act of feeding the multitude, the Father's presence and power and his approval of Jesus had been expressed.) They asked what they must do to do the work God wanted of them (vs. 28). Jesus said: Believe in him whom God has sent (vs. 29); they should believe in Jesus.

The people asked Jesus to do a sign to prove to them that he was the one in whom they should believe (vs. 30). This sounds strange. He had just fed the five thousand in a miraculous way; that, we may think, should have been sign enough. But they wanted something more. Moses had fed the Israelites with manna in the wilderness (vs. 31; see Exod. 16:13-30; Num. 11:7-9; Joshua 5:12); Psalms 78:24 and 105:40 could be quoted to recall that. There was a rabbinical expectation that when the Christ, the Greater Moses, came he would feed his people in an even more remarkable way. The crowd, it seems, was saying: If you claim to be that greater leader in whom we should believe, do the expected greater miracle as the sign that you are what you claim to be.

In reply Jesus said two things (vss. 32-33): (1) It was not Moses but God who gave that manna to Israel; God is the source of man's blessings. (2) Man's real food is not physical food—necessary as that is for physical life—but the bread from heaven which God gives to bestow and maintain true life; this is the food which every believer receives to sustain him in fellowship with God and in loyalty to God's will. The people see that Jesus refers to spiritual food, and ask that they may always have it as his gift to them (vs. 34). In calling him "Lord" they indicate not crafty courtesy but at least a tentative faith in him.

Jesus now comes to his central point. He is "the bread of life" (vss. 35, 48); he can satisfy man's hunger and thirst for God and for true life, so that man's every need is always met (Matt. 5:6). Jesus has been offering this food to men but they have not accepted it; they have not really believed in him (vs. 36). This rejection has not happened by chance. Though each person must answer to God for his own decision, the failure of hearers to believe has a deeper explanation: God has marked out those who are to believe, and they all will come to Jesus, that is, believe in him, and he will reject none of them (vs. 37). The others God has not given to him, and since Jesus has come to do the will of the Father who sent him into the world (vs. 38), he accepts the wisdom of this mysterious divine plan, and makes it his constant concern to win to faith, train in obedience, and keep safe all whom the Father has given him (vs. 39; 17:12). Although physical death may overtake them before the last day, he will raise them on that day and thus, acting for God, give them the privilege of full, perfect eternal life in the eternal time to come. This is the Father's will, that every person who sees the divine Son in the human Jesus and believes in him should have eternal life, beginning at once and perfected in permanent and unhindered expression at the last day (vs. 40). In essence this life is available now to every believer (3:36); but in unchallenged perfection it will be given at the last day.

The persistent hostility and skepticism of most Jewish hearers emerge again (vs. 41). How does this claim to be the bread which has come down from heaven square with facts they know (vs. 42), that Jesus came from a humble though good home, of known human parents (as was commonly thought), in an unimportant town of Galilee? In view of his humble origin, they think he claims far too much.

Jesus repeats in verse 44 the point of verse 37; faith is not an independent human work for which man gets credit. God, who has sent Jesus, draws men to Jesus and prompts them to believe, and Jesus, sent by God, will raise up such believers at the last day; from beginning to end man's salvation is God's planning and God's work, centered in Jesus. Jesus finds this expressed in Isaiah 54:13; only as men are "taught by God" and learn from the Father do they come to Jesus in faith (vs. 45). And it is Jesus, only Jesus, who has really seen and lived with the Father in closest fellowship and so can make him known (vs. 46; compare 1:18; 14:8-11). This does not deny the Old Testament revelation and God's use of prophets, but it centers God's revelation in the Son and implies that, as 1:4 and 1:9 say, all revelation comes through the Word or Son of God, whose work centers in his earthly career but extends over the entire sweep of man's history. So whoever believes in him has eternal life (vs. 47), for he has found the one way to real and full life (14:6); Jesus is the Bread of Life (vss. 35, 48) and meets every need of those who believe in and abide in him (ch. 15).

This food which Jesus gives far surpasses what the manna gave; if the crowd expects his work to surpass that of Moses, they will find their expectations fulfilled if they believe. Those who ate the manna died in the wilderness (vs. 49), and thus had only a temporary physical benefit from it. But the food which Jesus gives to believers will sustain them in true life with God now and for all time to come (vs. 50); Jesus the living Bread not only lives himself but also gives to all who believe in him life that continues safe and blessed forever (vs. 51a).

A new and much disputed point comes in when Jesus says that this bread which he will give to give life to the world is his flesh (vs. 51b). This sounds to the hearers like cannibalism (vs. 52). Jesus makes the saying still more offensive by adding that they must not only eat his flesh but drink his blood (vs. 53). To Jews, forbidden by their Law to drink blood (Lev. 3:17; 7:26; 17:10-14), this was shocking language. To make eternal life depend on eating his flesh and drinking his blood (vs. 54), to say that this flesh and blood is the believer's real food (vs. 55), to make fellowship with Jesus depend on such eating (vss. 56-57), to say that his physical flesh and blood give life as the ancient manna could not do (vs. 58)—all this was shocking and contrary to Jewish teaching, yet it was said in the synagogue at Capernaum (vs. 59), where the Law of Moses was regularly read and taught as the basis for community worship and life. If this was meant literally, it was a radical break with Judaism.

"The Jews" (vss. 41, 52)—the crowd who at first were inclined to be favorable (vss. 14, 24, 34) but later became more skeptical and murmured at him (vs. 41)—now fade from view. Some of the disciples themselves began to object (vs. 60). They could not accept Jesus' "hard saying" about eating his flesh and drinking his blood. They murmured in private, but Jesus knew what they were saying and answered them (vs. 61). We have to remember

here the frequent teaching method of this Gospel—giving an ambiguous statement, then giving the objection of the hearers, and
finally showing what Jesus really meant by giving his reply to
the objection. His reply here indicates that his meaning was not
crassly physical but was more spiritual than they had understood.
They will see the Son of Man ascending to the Father, with whom
he, the Word, was in close fellowship before he became flesh
(vs. 62; see 1:1, 14). After his ascension he will not be physically present with his disciples in such fashion that they can really
eat his flesh and drink his blood. The spirit, not the flesh, gives
life; his words are spirit and life; the disciples will get the food he
promises if they hear his words, grasp their message, believe in
him, and abide in him even when he is exalted to the Father by
being lifted up on the cross (vs. 63).

Thus Jesus ended this discussion not by insisting that the disciples must eat his physical flesh and drink his physical blood, but
by stating the spiritual truth hidden in those strong words. The
Word became flesh. His earthly career was absolutely basic and
decisive for salvation; not only his words but his death on the
cross (1:29) was for men's salvation. This is not merely a reference to the Lord's Supper, as is usually thought. It is a statement
that the believer's entire life of faith, worship, fellowship, and
obedience depends on Jesus and on what Jesus has done for his
people by his life and death. The Lord's Supper recalls and expresses that fact, but so does every true act of worship and obedience to Christ.

Jesus knew that even among his disciples (vs. 60) there were
some who did not really believe in him (vs. 64). He knew who
they were. Their failure to continue with him did not surprise or
discourage him; he even knew who would betray him (vss. 70-
71). He shared such secret knowledge with the Father, without
whose gracious choice and leading no one can come to Jesus and
be saved (vs. 65). But the purpose of God is steadfast, and nothing will stop its steady and complete realization.

The conflict between faith and unbelief thus reached into the
very circle of Jesus' disciples. Many left him (vs. 66); they were
not ready to make the complete and grateful commitment which
he required of those who were to receive the final gift of eternal
life. The Twelve, here mentioned for the first time (vs. 67), remained faithful, though even among them was one man who
would betray Jesus (vs. 71).

Jesus put them to the test: Did they want to leave him? As usual, Peter acted as their spokesman; it is understood that the others approved his words (perhaps even Judas did; perhaps he did not know yet where the seeds of doubt would finally lead him). In faith Peter said that for him and the other loyal disciples the one source of the words and gift of eternal life was Jesus (vs. 68). The Twelve had put their faith in him and by living as his disciples had come to know with steady assurance that he was "the Holy One of God" (vs. 69; compare Mark 1:24; Luke 4:34). This is the closest this Gospel comes to paralleling the confession of Jesus as the Christ which Peter makes at the climax of Jesus' public ministry in Mark 8:29; Matthew 16:16; and Luke 9:20 (but see 1:41). This confession does not identify Jesus as the expected Christ; rather, it describes him as consecrated by God for his unique ministry. It implies that he alone can give the truth, redemptive grace, and power necessary for salvation and obedient living.

Jesus did not comment on Peter's confession, except to point out that the failure to believe reached into the very circle of the Twelve (vss. 70-71). Jesus himself had chosen them, and yet one of them he described as "a devil"; that one was already responding to the Devil's leading and serving the Devil's purposes. Jesus knew that Judas would betray him, but there is no sign that Peter or others of the Twelve knew it, and it is not certain that Judas already knew clearly what he would finally do. More than once in this Gospel men start on the way of faith and yet, for lack of full knowledge and steady faithfulness, fail to come to complete dedication and so in the end actually reject Jesus and serve evil.

Jesus the Light of the World Meeting Life Danger (7:1—9:41)

In 6:59 Jesus is in Galilee, at Capernaum. Now in 7:1 he travels about in Galilee. This is the last time this Gospel mentions a ministry in Galilee, which Jesus leaves for the last time in verse 10. Even here, the ministry is mentioned mainly as a withdrawal from Judea to avoid danger there; as 5:18 said, hostile Jews had plans against his life. That point is repeated in 7:1, 19, 25; 8:37, 40. Jesus will die in Jerusalem, but only when the divinely appointed hour has come. Chapter 7 tells nothing of what Jesus did in Galilee; verses 2-10 imply a Galilean ministry but serve mainly to prepare for the return to Jerusalem.

The Feast of Tabernacles (Lev. 23:33-43; Deut. 16:13-15)

was at hand (vs. 2). This fall festival, celebrated after all the
year's crops, including the grapes, had been harvested, recalled
the unsettled, homeless life of the children of Israel in the wilderness after they were delivered from Egypt. It was one of the three
great festival seasons of the year (the other two were Passover-
Unleavened Bread and Pentecost). Great crowds of loyal Jews
would make special pilgrimage to Jerusalem. So Jesus' brothers
urged him to go to Judea, that is, to Jerusalem, and there do
openly the works he had been doing in Galilee (vs. 3). Such
things, the brothers said, should be done publicly, before the
world (vs. 4), to confirm his disciples whom he already had. The
brothers were not urging him to make new disciples; they themselves did not believe in him (vs. 5), though they admitted that
he had done remarkable deeds. The wider spread of his message
was not their concern; they were taunting Jesus for being afraid
to test his powers in Jerusalem.

There are three views as to the parents of these brothers, who
are named in Matthew 13:55 and Mark 6:3. On one view, since
Jesus was Mary's first-born son (Matt. 1:25; Luke 2:7), they are
sons of Joseph and Mary, born after the birth of Jesus. Another
widely held view is that they were sons of Joseph by a former
wife, and so not sons of Mary at all. Still a third view is that
"brothers" here means "cousins"; the so-called "brothers" were
only cousins of Jesus. The first of the three views seems to be the
one suggested by the Bible passages.

Jesus refused to go to Jerusalem in response to the brothers'
challenge. He never let others tell him what to do; he lived with
the constant awareness that the Father had a fixed plan and time
for each stage of his work. When his brothers urged him to go to
Jerusalem, he did not yet feel that his hour had come to go to
Jerusalem and face whatever might happen there (vs. 6). The
brothers might go at once; their life was not governed by the
divine plan. Indeed, since they did not believe in Jesus and thus
were in sympathy with the world hostile to Jesus, their movements had no constructive place in God's plan and would arouse
no such hate as Jesus' ministry had met. But one question remains.
What did Jesus say about not going? According to some manuscripts, his words in verse 8 were, "I am *not* going up to the
feast"; but according to other manuscripts he said, "I am *not yet*
going up to the feast." It is impossible to be certain which reading is original. In either case, Jesus refused to go up for the full

length of the feast, and he waited until he knew that it was the Father's will for him to go.

When he knew that, Jesus went, not with his brothers and not in the public throngs which went in time to reach Jerusalem before the feast began, but alone or accompanied only by close friends (vs. 10). Evidently many pilgrims had come in hope of seeing him, and though the officials were known to be opposed to him and the people were afraid to discuss him openly (vs. 13), they talked much about him in low voices (vss. 11-12). Opinions were divided: some thought him a good man, helpful in word and act; others thought him a bad influence, leading people astray from the true Jewish faith and worship.

In the middle of the feast, about the fourth day, Jesus suddenly appeared in the crowded Temple court and taught boldly (vs. 14). His skill and power in teaching amazed the hearers, especially since all knew that he had not had special training (vs. 15).

Jesus' teaching here included several points: (1) What he says is not his own invention; the Father who has sent him has given him his message (vs. 16). (2) Whoever honestly determines to do the Father's will and faithfully obeys Jesus' teaching will know without doubt that his teaching is God-given (vs. 17) and that he is sincerely and obediently working to lead men to praise and honor God (vs. 18). (3) Jesus agrees that Moses gave Israel the Law, but he indicts his hearers, as Stephen does later in Acts 7:53, for not keeping it (vs. 19). (4) Going back to the hostile reaction of the Jews when he healed the sick man on the Sabbath (5:18), Jesus asks why they, who do not keep the Law, try to kill him for an alleged violation of the law about the Sabbath (vs. 19). Though they deny any intent to kill him (vs. 20), he persists in his criticism. He did "one deed," that is, healed the sick man (ch. 5). They marvel at it (vs. 21), but do not believe in him; they rather are angry at him (vs. 23), charging that his healing breaks the Sabbath. (In 5:8-10 the healed man carried his pallet; this was what was said to break the Sabbath, but this was done at Jesus' command, so he could be blamed if it was wrong.)

Jesus goes on to show that one duty may be so important that it temporarily cancels another one. The Law says to do no work on the Sabbath. But it also says to circumcise a child on the eighth day of his life (Lev. 12:3), and interpreters of the Law agreed that if the eighth day was a Sabbath, the work of circumcision should be done regardless of the law against work on the

Sabbath. (Jesus notes in passing that circumcision antedates the time of Moses; Genesis 17:10 and 21:4 show that it was practiced by the "fathers," that is, the patriarchs.) So on the Jewish understanding of the Law it was wrong to condemn him for healing a man on the Sabbath (vss. 22-23). He did it to give normal life to a fellow man. He was doing God's will by helping one of God's children. Right judgment would lead them to approve his action (vs. 24). The other Gospels show that for Jesus, "The sabbath was made for man, not man for the sabbath" (Mark 2:27); when he met human suffering or need on the Sabbath, he was ready to heal and give the needy person health and normal life.

The people continued to be uncertain and divided. It was plain that the leaders, though they wanted to get rid of Jesus (5:18; 7:1, 19), were not stopping his public preaching (vs. 25). This failure of the leaders to act suggested to some that perhaps the leaders had reached the secret conviction that Jesus was the expected Messiah of the Jews (vs. 26). Then, continuing their chronic failure to understand that Jesus was sent by God as the full answer to all man's needs, and with complacent assurance that they knew all about Jesus, they said they knew where he came from (knew his home town and parents) but the Messiah would appear in so mysterious a way that no one would know whence he came (vs. 27). This latter idea was current among Jews. Jesus, in reply, asked whether they really knew him and his origin; he implied that though they thought they did, they really did not. And they did not know the Father who had sent him (vs. 28). Jesus knew him, came from him, and had been sent by him (vs. 29). Only by accepting Jesus as the Christ sent by God would they really know God.

A definite division now appeared among the people. Some tried to seize him to deliver him to the authorities because of his blasphemous claim to be the God-sent authoritative leader of Israel (vs. 30). But they could not thwart God's plan; when Jesus' hour to suffer came, he would be taken, but not before. Others believed in him (vs. 31), but with a limited and querulous faith. They recognized that Jesus' miracles were signs that God approved him, but they did not confess him to be their Christ; in fact, they spoke as if the coming of the Christ were still future. They still did not have the full faith which this Gospel was written to promote.

The attempt to seize Jesus (vs. 30) was evidently an unofficial action. When the Pharisees heard that some were inclined to believe in Jesus, they moved the Sanhedrin, which included chief priests and Pharisees, to send officers to arrest him (vs. 32). As verses 45-46 show, the officers found Jesus and listened to him but did not seize him.

Jesus went on teaching, but warned the people that his remaining time for public teaching was short; he would soon return to the Father who sent him, and then they would not be able to find him or follow him (vss. 33-34). They did not understand that he soon would be exalted to honor and fellowship with the Father. They thought that perhaps he meant to go to the Dispersion (vs. 35)—that is, to the Jews living in Gentile lands—and teach not only those Jews, most of whom would speak Greek, but also the "Greeks," that is, the Gentiles, in those lands. To the Gospel writer these words of verse 35 were pointing to the Gentile mission that was destined to come. But the crowd hearing Jesus were not sure what he meant (vs. 36). He referred to his essential tie with the Father, but they did not understand him. Yet that was just what they needed to understand for their own spiritual understanding and salvation; to understand his vital bond with the Father would lead them to believe in him and so to find life through that faith.

At the Feast of Tabernacles it was the custom on the first day, and perhaps on each day of the feast, to carry a pitcher of water up to the Temple from the spring at the foot of the Temple hill. This festive ceremony was connected with prayer for the fall and winter rains which would ensure crops during the coming spring and summer. Perhaps it was with this ceremony in mind that Jesus, on the final day of the feast (vs. 37), took his stand in a prominent public place, no doubt in the Temple court as in verse 14, and urged the (spiritually) thirsty to come to him and drink (see Matt. 5:6). To drink, that is, to quench spiritual thirst, one must believe in Jesus as the Christ sent of God. He who believes will then have in himself a spring or source of living (flowing and life-giving) water (vs. 38). He will have a constant, divinely given life and outgoing power.

This promise is said to fulfill the Scripture; no Old Testament passage says just what is here quoted, but the idea occurs in Isaiah 44:3 and 55:1. The promise of water and the Spirit in Isaiah 44:3 is recalled by the added statement that the living water refers to the presence and action of the Holy Spirit in the believer (vs. 39). The life and power of the believer are not his own achievement but are the gift of the Spirit.

The Gospel writer notes that the Spirit had not been given as yet (vs. 39). In this Gospel he was given on the evening of the Resurrection day (20:22). In a sense the Spirit of God had been present and active in the world since the Creation (Gen. 1:2), but the Spirit as believers know him, continuing the work of Christ and interpreting that work to the Christian, could be given only after the earthly work of Jesus had been completed.

The division apparent in verses 11-12 and 30-31 reappears in verses 40-44. Four groups emerge: (1) Those who decided that Jesus was the great prophet promised in Deuteronomy 18:15, 18 (vs. 40). (2) Those who confessed that Jesus was the expected Christ (vs. 41a). (3) Those skeptics who denied that Jesus could be the Christ (vss. 41b-42). They expected the Christ to be the Son of David from Bethlehem, David's home city. They did not know the story of Jesus' birth at Bethlehem (some doubt that the Gospel writer did, but probably he did, and simply did not pause to correct the crowd's misunderstanding). They knew only that he had lived at Nazareth in Galilee, so they concluded that he did not fit the promise in Micah 5:2 and could not be the Christ. (4) Those who thought Jesus so misguided and dangerous to Jewish faith that they wanted him arrested (vs. 44). But as in verse 30 and elsewhere, his hour had not yet come, and he could not be arrested until his ministry was ended. Even though officers from the Sanhedrin were present, and had been sent to seize him, this desire for his arrest went unfulfilled.

When the officers returned to the Sanhedrin without the prisoner and were asked why they had not obeyed orders to arrest him (vs. 45), they testified to the matchless gripping power of Jesus' teaching (vs. 46). In scorn and rebuke the leaders pointed out that none of the leaders had believed in Jesus (but see 12:42); the common people, they declared with contemptuous condemnation, were not competent to decide whether Jesus' teaching agreed with the Law (vss. 47-49). The leaders could not realize that they were blindly missing their spiritual opportunity to find life through Jesus, and that some of the common people were more open than they were to God's appeal.

Nicodemus, a Sanhedrin member who early had stated that he and others recognized Jesus as a teacher come from God (3:2),

objected to condemning Jesus before he had been given a hearing
(vss. 50-51). This principle was implicit in the Law's standards
of fairness, and was evidently accepted in Jewish circles in Jesus'
day. But the leaders were too blinded by hostility to be fair.
They witheringly asked Nicodemus whether he, too, was from
Galilee, as Jesus was; their meaning was, Are you, too, a follower
of this misguided Galilean teacher? They added that the Scripture
promised no prophet from Galilee (vs. 52). Jonah was from
Gath-hepher in Galilee (see II Kings 14:25), but the Jewish
leaders may have meant that the great final prophet and leader
whom God had promised for the future (Deut. 18:15, 18) would
come from Bethlehem, as Micah 5:2 was taken to mean, or at
least from Judea. Since, as far as they knew, Jesus was from
Galilee, and they knew nothing of his birth at Bethlehem, they
rejected him. He did not come in the way Scripture had said he
would, so he could not be God's special prophet and Messiah.
(Obviously the birth stories found in Matthew 1-2 and Luke 1-2
were not publicly known during Jesus' ministry.)

The story of the woman taken in adultery (7:53—8:11), so
well known today, was not part of the original Gospel of John.
The earliest and best manuscripts do not contain it. Later manuscripts which have it differ as to where they place it. One manuscript puts it after 7:36; a few put it after 21:25; others put it
after Luke 21:38; most of those which have it put it after John
7:52. The manuscripts which have it also vary greatly in the
wording of the passage. The vocabulary and Greek style of the
passage differ from those of the Gospel of John. This story was a
loose bit of tradition which was inserted in the Gospel at a later
time to keep it from being lost. Does it report a real event in
the life of Jesus? Possibly so. While it contains no confession
of sin by the woman and no direct word of forgiveness by Jesus,
it does express his sympathy for sinners and his insistence that
outwardly pious people need to repent of their own sin before
they condemn obvious sinners.

The story represents Jesus as in Jerusalem. Verses 10 and 25
of chapter 7 show that Jesus was there at the end of chapter 7, so
this passage could be inserted at this point in John. After ending
a day of teaching (7:53), Jesus spent the night on the Mount of
Olives (7:53—8:1). The next morning, as Jesus taught in the
Temple area (vs. 2), a woman caught in the act of adultery was
brought to him (vs. 3). Why the guilty man was not brought is

not clear; if both guilty parties were married, Leviticus 20:10 would prescribe death for him as well as for the woman, but it does not say how the two should be put to death. Deuteronomy 22:21-22 prescribes stoning for a bride found at marriage to have had immoral relations with a man at some earlier time, but it does not specify stoning in the case of a married woman caught committing adultery.

The scribes and Pharisees in this passage used the woman to test Jesus (vss. 4-6). If he said not to stone her, he could be condemned as a rebel against the Law of Moses. If he said to stone her, he would lose the popular following which his sympathy and helpfulness to wrongdoers had won for him. His reply in effect asked, Which one of you is morally perfect, free from fault, and really qualified to judge your fellow Jew? Whoever is without sin may go ahead and stone the woman (vs. 7). His writing on the ground, both before and after saying this (vss. 6, 8), was to give them time to think what they were doing. They could not claim to be perfect; they did not dare to take up the challenge. One by one they went away, beginning with the oldest, who presumably must act as leader and also could know best how imperfect man's obedience to God is (vs. 9). Jesus did not condemn the woman; he assumed that she felt shame, and the implication is that he forgave her. He did not mean to promote immorality by dealing gently with her, so he warned her not to sin again but to lead a life of moral integrity from that time on (vss. 10-11).

Chapter 8:12-59 continues, it seems, Jesus' teaching on the last day of the Feast of Tabernacles (7:37). He was "in the treasury" (8:20), in the Court of Women of the Temple. At that feast, lights were lit in the Court of Women on the first night, and quite likely on the other nights of the feast. Possibly this suggested to Jesus the use of the illustration of light, for he knew himself to be "the light of men" (1:4), "the light of the world," giving not only intellectual understanding but especially the spiritual light needed to reveal God to men (Ps. 36:9). He thus picks up and embodies what Isaiah 9:1-2 and 60:1-3 say about the light God has promised his people. Without that light man walks in moral and spiritual darkness; with it, he knows his way and enjoys God-given life. Chapter 9 will take up and illustrate this truth.

The Pharisees, chief opponents of Jesus' teaching, challenged his claim (vs. 13). In their legal system, as they pointed out, a man's words about himself were not valid testimony. Indeed, Jesus himself recognized a truth in this (5:31); others must verify whatever a man says on his own behalf. But in another sense Jesus could say that his words about his ministry were true; he knew and could testify to his divine origin and his coming exaltation to the Father, while his opponents did not know his origin or destiny (vs. 14). Besides, they judged by fleshly, that is, human and worldly, standards. Jesus' real aim was not to condemn people but to save them (3:17), so he could say that he did not judge; but when he did pronounce judgment, it was a true and just judgment, for he never acted alone but always spoke in full accord with the mind and will of the Father who had sent him into the world to save men (vss. 15-16). So Jesus answered the Pharisees in legal style; if they appealed to the Law, which required at least two witnesses to verify a point (Deut. 19:15), he could say that he and the Father both witnessed to the mission and claim of Jesus (vss. 17-18).

The Pharisees then asked, "Where is your Father?" That is: If you offer two witnesses, let us see the other one; you say the Father is your witness; where is he? In other words, you after all are the only witness we see, and you cannot testify alone in your own behalf and expect us to listen to you. Jesus replied that they did not know him or his Father. They did not know who he was and that he was God-sent, and they did not really know the God they professed to worship. And since Jesus was the Way (14:6), it was only by knowing him and accepting him by faith as the Word made flesh, the Christ, the Son of God, that they would truly come to know the Father (vs. 19). They remained unconvinced, but they could not seize him or harm him yet, for his hour to complete his earthly ministry by death had not yet come, and sinful men could not thwart or destroy the divine plan for his life and work (vs. 20).

The time for Jesus' departure from this earthly life had not come, but it was near. He would soon go away; then they would sense their need and seek him for help, but it would be too late. There would come a time when it would be too late to accept God's free offer; they would not be able to follow him and get the needed help (vs. 21). They did not understand; how could he escape them so completely? By suicide? They could think only of that (vs. 22). Ignoring this mistaken suggestion, he hinted strongly of his divine origin (vs. 23); he was not of merely hu-

man origin nor involved in sin as they were, but was from above
and could save them from their sins if they would only believe
in him. But he saw no real prospect that they would believe, so
he saw only spiritual death, final and complete ruin, ahead for
them (vs. 24).

To this assertion that they must believe in him or face ruin,
they replied, "Who are you?" (vs. 25). It is not certain just what
the first words of his response mean. The Greek words may be
translated either (1) "Basically, I am just what I am telling you,"
or (2) "I am just what I have been telling you from the beginning," or (3) "Why do I talk to you at all?" In any case,
Jesus declared that he had much more to say about them and to
judge in them, and it was true and dependable for it came from
the One who sent him. That One was always true, and Jesus was
teaching exactly what he had been sent to say (vs. 26).

The hearers did not understand that Jesus was speaking of the
Father as the One who had sent him and given him his message
(vs. 27), so he went on to say this clearly, and promised that
when they had lifted him up on the cross, they would know that
he was God-sent (vs. 28). He added that the Father was always
with him and never left him alone, and that he always did what
the Father wanted him to do (vs. 29). To this clear claim that
his words and acts were inspired by the Father and faithfully
followed the Father's will, many of the hearers responded by
believing (vs. 30). But this was not a full and sturdy faith. As
the discussion went further and they understood better the full
scope of the gospel message, they drew back and Jesus actually
condemned them (vs. 44).

What did these new believers still need? They must continue
in Jesus' teaching by keeping it alive in their memory and obeying it. Then they would be true disciples, true *learners* and followers (this is what the word "disciples" means); they would
know ever more fully the truth about God, God's will, man's
need, and God's gifts to believers; and that truth, accepted,
obeyed, and gratefully cherished, would make them free (vss. 31-
32). Free? That implied that without the gospel they were slaves.
This they denied. They were descendants of Abraham. Their
people, to be sure, had been defeated and subjugated by foreign
rulers, but their patriotic spirit had not been broken; they had not
accepted inwardly the position of slaves; they had always been
free (vs. 33).

But they had the wrong idea of freedom. Jesus spoke of slavery to sin (vs. 34). People often think that to be free means to do as they please, to do wrong without qualms of conscience. Jesus knew that wrongdoing takes away freedom, enslaves men to bad ways of acting, and while promising freedom and happiness actually brings slavery and frustration. The wrongdoer becomes a slave to sin. No slave really belongs to the family of the household he serves; only the son of the family belongs with permanent family status (vs. 35). So if man wants to be free, he can be so only when he is a son; since men have sinned, one becomes free only when, by the work of Christ, the Son of God, he is made a son of the Father and is received among the children of God; then he will be really and permanently free as he lives with the Father and the Son (vs. 36).

Jesus admitted that the Jews who were arguing with him were physically descended from Abraham, but spiritually Abraham was not their father. Jesus had told them what he had heard from God his Father, and they did not accept his words as Abraham and his true descendants would do (vs. 37). So they had another father (vs. 38)—not God, not Abraham (see vs. 44). They still stubbornly insisted that they were descended from Abraham, and so could call him their father (vs. 39). Jesus replied that to be sons of Abraham meant to live with Abraham's obedience and responsiveness to God's promises and action (see vs. 56); since they did not do that, but rather tried to kill Jesus for teaching the gospel message he had heard from God, they showed that spiritually they were not Abraham's children (vss. 39-40). They were following the pattern of another who was their spiritual father, their real object of worship and obedience (vs. 41).

They retorted that they had not been following other gods (the word "fornication" was used in the Old Testament to refer to worship of other gods instead of being faithful to God alone); their one Father, they claimed, was God; their spiritual loyalty was to him alone (vs. 41). That, Jesus said, was not true; if it were, they would love him (vs. 42). God had sent him and he came from God to save them, but they did not listen to and accept his message (vs. 43). They could not, he added, because their real loyalty was to the Devil; he was their father, and they stood ready to do his wishes (vs. 44). Since the Devil wanted to defeat the purpose of Jesus and put Jesus out of the way, he

wanted them to kill Jesus and they were ready to do so. The
Devil had always been active in murder, and since he was a
liar by nature and had no loyalty to the truth, he spoke and
lived lies and promoted lies. That was his constant business.
People who were serving the Devil therefore could not understand or accept Jesus, who was telling the truth about God, God's
will, man's need, and God's gifts to men of faith (vs. 45).

To sharpen the point, Jesus challenged his hearers: Which of
them could point to and prove the presence of sin in him? Why
did they not believe him when he was telling the truth? (vs. 46).
It could only be because they were not God's children; God's
children listen to the words of God, and since Jesus was speaking
God's word, God's children would listen to and accept Jesus
(vs. 47).

But these Jews blamed Jesus. He was a Samaritan, they said
(vs. 48); he was false to the God of Israel, just as the Samaritans—so the Jews believed—had given themselves to the worship
of other gods and so stood outside the People of God. He had a
demon: it was not God's Spirit but the power of evil that indwelt,
controlled, and directed him (see Mark 3:22). This charge Jesus
could truthfully deny; he honored his Father by teaching and
acting according to God's will, yet they dishonored him by rejecting Jesus' message and appeal (vs. 49). His aim was not to
promote his own reputation and standing; the Father would
vindicate him and establish his place of honor. The Father,
Jesus implied, would judge and condemn all who refused to give
the Son the honor which the Father had decreed for him (vs. 50).
The message which Jesus had received from the Father and faithfully delivered was so crucial that whoever would accept it and
remain faithful to it would never see death (vs. 51). By "death"
Jesus meant here, as in chapter 11, final and complete spiritual
ruin due to sinful disobedience to God in rejecting Jesus' message.
But as so often, his hearers misunderstood. They thought he
meant physical death and was claiming that none of his followers
would ever suffer such death; they thought that such an absurd
claim, made although even Abraham and the prophets had died,
showed that Jesus was mentally unbalanced, under the influence
of an evil demon (vss. 52-53).

Jesus said that he would not anxiously defend himself; the
Father would vindicate him. They were not loyal and obedient to
the Father, as they claimed to be, but he was faithfully keeping

(obeying) his Father's word (vss. 54-55). Then he referred again to Abraham, the father of Israel, who had been accepted by both sides as an example of true faith and loyalty to God. Abraham, Jesus said, saw the day of Jesus' coming and ministry, and rejoiced that the fulfillment of God's promise was surely coming (vs. 56).

How old was Jesus when this debate occurred? The hostile Jews said he was not yet fifty. The only other hint as to his age during his ministry is Luke 3:23, which says that when his ministry began he was about thirty; this is probably a more dependable clue to his actual age than John 8:57, which only means that Jesus was no more than a middle-aged man and so could not possibly have known Abraham. Jesus had not said that he knew Abraham; he said that Abraham saw (foresaw) his day (vs. 56). But Jesus drew their attention to the eternal existence of the Word who had recently become flesh. Speaking with the formula of emphasis—"Truly, truly, I say to you"—which this Gospel uses for important statements, Jesus said, "Before Abraham was, I am" (vs. 58). He thus spoke of his continuous existence in such a way as to imply that he did not begin to exist at any time but was always in existence, even before Abraham or any other figure of man's earliest history. "In the beginning was the Word" (1:1). We may go back as far as the biblical story goes, and the Word is there, already existing, with no date of beginning.

The words of verse 58 were an obvious claim of divine nature and dignity. The hearers, again indignant at this supposedly blasphemous claim to divine nature, were roused to stone Jesus, but he hid himself—just how, whether by mingling with the milling crowd or by the divine power he possessed, is not said—and left the Temple court where the discussion had taken place (vs. 59). The conflict between Jesus' claim and the world's hostility continued; the climax was yet to come.

In the story of the man born blind (9:1-41), Jesus was in Jerusalem (7:10, 14; 8:20). After leaving the Temple (8:59), he saw a beggar (9:8) who had been blind from birth (vs. 1). He gave sight to this man to show that he is the Light of the world (8:12; 9:5), who gives spiritual light and leading to those who have been in the darkness of sin. But to his disciples the blind man suggested a different question (vs. 2). They shared the common idea (which Job's friends had shared much earlier!) that physical misfortune is punishment for sin. So they asked him,

their Teacher and Master, whose sin it was which explained this
blindness from birth. Did the man's parents commit some great
sin, for which their son's blindness was the punishment, the sin
of the parents being visited on their child? (Exod. 34:7). Or did
the man himself in some mysterious way sin even before he was
born, and receive blindness from birth as penalty?

As in Luke 13:1-5, Jesus denied that physical misfortune is
certain proof of the sufferer's special sinfulness. He did not say
whether the man or his parents had sinned, though since he
taught all followers to pray daily for forgiveness (Matt. 6:12),
he could have said that they had. He focused on the real meaning
of the occasion. It gave him an opportunity to make God's power
and purpose clear through the healing he was now to perform
(vs. 3).

The darkness in which blindness had kept the man led Jesus
to describe the time of his own ministry as a "day" in which he
must do promptly what his Father had sent him to do. Just as
men must do their work before darkness falls, so he had to act
at once when the need appeared, before the fixed time for his
ministry passed (vs. 4). Repeating his earlier announcement
(8:12), he emphasized that during his earthly ministry he was the
Light of the world (vs. 5). Then he healed the blind man to
symbolize the light-bringing effect of his ministry. The healing
was a real physical healing, but it symbolized the spiritual illumi-
nation Jesus gives to those who open their eyes to him and his
work.

Jesus spat on the dusty ground and so made clay with which
to smear the eyes of the blind man (vs. 6). In ancient times
spittle was thought to have healing power, so perhaps here it
symbolized the healing purpose of Jesus. Only here and in Mark
7:33 and 8:23 did Jesus in healing use such a physical help as
spittle; elsewhere he at most placed his hand on the sick person
to strengthen faith and confidence. The blind man was put to the
test: he was told to go to the pool of Siloam (the name is explained as coming from a Hebrew word meaning "sent") and
wash; he had to have some faith to be willing to do this, and
when he showed this faith, he received his sight (vs. 7). The
Light of the world had taken away the darkness in which he had
been living.

The man was a well-known figure; being blind, he could not
work for a living, so he had been a beggar, and many people, in-

cluding his neighbors, knew him (vs. 8). But his ability to see so surprised them that some doubted he was the same man (vs. 9). When he said that he was, they still hesitated, and asked how he could now see (vs. 10). When he told them who healed him and how (vs. 11), they asked where Jesus was, as though they had to question Jesus to check the story; but the man had lost touch with his benefactor (vs. 12). All this emphasizes how amazing it was for a man born blind to receive sight.

The skeptical neighbors and friends took the healed man to the Pharisees, who were generally recognized authorities on the Jewish Law and way of life (vs. 13). Then a new question emerged. The man had been healed on a Sabbath (vs. 14), and the act of making the clay, smearing the man's eyes, and washing the eyes might be considered work. Verses 15-34 tell how the Pharisees, even more persistently skeptical than the man's neighbors and friends, tried to evade the obvious fact that Jesus had really given the man his sight and so must have divine approval and power. But as soon as they asked and were told how sight was given (vs. 15), a division appeared among them. (Throughout the Gospel, Jesus forces every group to decide for or against him, and division appears in both the crowds and the group of Jewish leaders.) Some argued that a man who did not observe the Sabbath as Jewish Law and tradition prescribed must be a sinner. Others replied that a man who could do such signs as healing lifelong blindness could not be condemned as a sinner (vs. 16); such beneficent power, actively at work to help people, pointed to God's presence and power in Jesus—and this is what the Gospel writer wants the reader to see. The Pharisees, thus divided, asked the man his view of Jesus. In verse 11 he had simply called his healer "the man called Jesus"; in verse 17 he confessed that Jesus was "a prophet." This was a stage in his advance to full faith (see vs. 38).

In the light of verse 13, "the Jews" in verse 18 must be the Pharisees, especially those who considered Jesus a sinner (vs. 16). They suspected that the entire story of the healing was a fraud. So they called the parents from their home in Jerusalem and asked whether this man was really their son and had been born blind, and if so, how he had gained his sight (vss. 18-19). The parents were cautious, unwilling to get more involved in the dispute than was necessary; they admitted that the man was their son and was born blind, but professed not to know how he had received his

sight (vss. 20-21). They probably knew more than they said;
since the neighbors saw the healed man (vs. 8) he must have returned home, and so his parents must have heard his story of his
healing. But they declined to say so; the man was of age, and the
Jewish leaders could ask him. (Probably there was irony in their
reply; they must have known that the leaders had already asked
him and had heard the man tell his story!) They were cautious,
verse 22 says, because they knew that the Jewish leaders were
determined to crush any attempt to identify Jesus as the Christ
expected by the Jewish people. These leaders had decided to expel
from the synagogue and Jewish fellowship any person who confessed Jesus to be the Christ. This implies that the people in Jerusalem were discussing who Jesus really was, and the leaders were
vigorously opposing a tendency to confess Jesus to be the Messiah.

The parents had verified the facts: the man had been born
blind; in some remarkable way he had received his sight. But the
Jewish leaders were not satisfied. They could not prove the story
to be a fraud, but they would not admit that the healing had occurred. So they called the healed man again (vs. 24). Their command, "Give God the praise," meant, Tell the truth and so show
honor to the God of truth; tell us the real facts. And they added,
ignoring the objection of some of their number that a sinner
could not do such signs (vs. 16), that they knew Jesus was a sinner. The man declined to discuss that charge, although after con-
fessing Jesus to be a prophet sent by God (vs. 17), he could
hardly have agreed that Jesus was a sinner. He preferred to base
everything on the plain fact that Jesus had given him his sight;
he had been blind, and now could see (vs. 25). Before the leaders
could call Jesus a sinner, they must explain that undeniable
healing.

Their lack of any real answer came out in their next step (vs.
26); they asked again what they had already been told: how had
Jesus opened the man's eyes? Impatient at this stubborn refusal
to face facts, the man taunted them; since he had already told
them how the healing happened, did their desire to hear the story
again suggest that they wanted to become Jesus' disciples? (vs.
27). This enraged them (vs. 28). They denounced him as a disciple of Jesus (he had confessed some faith in verse 17, even
though not the full faith later expressed in verse 38); they were
proud to be disciples of Moses, true interpreters and followers
of the Mosaic Law (but see 5:46!). They knew, as every good

Jew knew, that God spoke to Moses; but they admitted and took pride in the fact that they did not know the origin of Jesus (vs. 29). Just so! This was their basic failure: Jesus had come to them from God, and they did not face this fact and confess it.

The man was quick to lay bare their blunder. Jesus had opened his eyes. Since he possessed the divine power to give sight to a blind man, he could not be a sinner. A man must have the power of God to do such signs; he must be a worshiper of God and a doer of God's will. God listens to such a man, and since God has listened to Jesus and enabled him to heal, Jesus must be a good man sent from God (vss. 30-31). The healing of a man born blind was unparalleled (vs. 32). The only possible explanation of so remarkable a deed was that God had sent Jesus and given him the power to do such things (vs. 33).

The leaders, taking up the explanation which Jesus had rejected in verse 3, replied that the man was born in sin; his parents were sinners, and his being born blind was due to that sin; he himself was continuing in sin; he could not be trusted to tell the truth, and yet he presumed to teach the religious leaders of his people (vs. 34). They "cast him out" of their meeting, or perhaps the meaning is that they expelled him from all participation in Jewish religious life. The irony is that they were the blind ones. They would not even admit that a powerful and beneficent healing had occurred; they could not see that Jesus had been sent by God; they accused the healed man of sin, but they themselves sinned in rejecting Jesus. Jesus later pointed this out to them (vss. 40-41).

But before that happened, Jesus brought the healed man to full faith. The man knew that Jesus was a prophet (vs. 17), sent by God (vs. 33). Jesus now found him and asked him whether he believed in the Son of man (vs. 35; some manuscripts read "Son of God" rather than "Son of man," but "Son of man" is probably what the Gospel writer wrote). "Son of man" here refers to Jesus as the incarnate divine messenger from God to men, bringing God's grace and truth to men and able to bring men to God. The title overlaps in meaning what the Gospel elsewhere means by saying "Son of God." The man at first did not see that Jesus was speaking of himself (vs. 36). (In all four Gospels the title "Son of man" is always used by Jesus himself, to refer to himself in his present ministry, impending suffering, future exaltation, and final judgment of mankind.) But when

Jesus made it clear that he was describing himself (vs. 37), the man at once addressed Jesus as his Lord. That he worshiped Jesus indicated his realization that God was present and active in Christ. He now understood who Jesus was and put his full faith in him (vs. 38).

Jesus closed the incident with a word about the judgment which his coming effected (vs. 39). Although he could truly say that he came not to judge the world but to save the world (3:17; 8:15; 12:47), it was also true that his coming placed men before a decision. Man cannot have the possibility of choosing life without the accompanying danger of condemnation and spiritual ruin if the offered gift is rejected. So here Jesus could say that he came for judgment, to give sight to those who were blind (provided they would believe and accept the gift), and to blind those who thought they could see but were unwilling to see that in him God was present to claim their loyalty and meet their need. Openness to Christ's help brings life, sight, and continual blessing; refusal to respond to his appeal deprives man of life, sight, and divine help, and leaves him spiritually blind and under divine judgment. There is no neutrality in life; there is every opportunity to receive every needed good, but there is always the danger of losing both present and future blessing by closing the eyes to the gift and privilege offered.

To this, some Pharisees asked incredulously, "Are we also blind?" (vs. 40). Jesus' reply meant: If you were really blind, and had had no chance to see and accept God's spiritual gifts in his Son, you would have no guilt; men are judged according to what they do with their opportunity. But you say you see; you claim to be spiritually enlightened and you feel no need of further light or help. In your complacent blindness to your need and to the greatness of the offer God makes in his Son, you turn from the light and ignore your opportunity. You know enough to know better, but you refuse to do what you should, so your sin remains (vs. 41). People who were satisfied with their spiritual condition were the ones of whom Jesus most despaired.

Jesus the Door and Good Shepherd (10:1-21)

Jesus was skillful in using illustrations from the life of his hearers. Since Palestine was familiar with the raising and care of sheep, it was natural for him to compare his care for his disciples with that which a shepherd gives his sheep. The Old Testament speaks of God (Isa. 40:11) or the king (Ps. 78:70-72) as shepherd of the people, and in other Gospels Jesus used this same "figure" (vs. 6; see Matt. 18:12-14; Luke 15:3-7). In John 21:16 Jesus says, "Tend my sheep," or, literally, "Shepherd my sheep." This reminds us that our word "pastor" comes from the Latin word for "shepherd" and describes a Christian minister as a shepherd.

The sheep were kept at night in a sheepfold, so that wild beasts and thieving men could not harm or steal them. The fold was surrounded by a wall and was entered by a gate or door guarded by a gatekeeper, who admitted only the shepherds whose flocks were kept in that fold. The shepherd to whom one of the flocks belonged would enter by the door when he wanted to see or get his sheep, and the gatekeeper would recognize him and open the door for him (vss. 2-3). Only a thief or robber would climb over the wall to get at the sheep (vs. 1). The sheep knew their shepherd; they trusted him. When they heard his voice, they recognized it, and when he called them to follow him out to pasture, they willingly followed (vs. 4). If a stranger came and called them, they were not deceived and would not follow (vs. 5); they knew the voice was not that of their shepherd. Verse 1 contrasts the true shepherd with thieves and robbers who climb into the sheepfold because their purpose is selfish and evil (see also vss. 8, 10); verse 5 contrasts the true shepherd with a stranger who tries to get the sheep to follow him but has no right to the sheep.

Since verse 1 begins abruptly, without connection with the preceding verses, it is not clear exactly when and where Jesus spoke this "figure" or illustration. Of course he was speaking to "the Jews" (vs. 19), and apparently he was at Jerusalem (see vss. 22-23). The Jews understood the illustration, for they knew well the relation of shepherd to sheep, but they did not understand just what point Jesus wanted to illustrate (vs. 6). Verses 7-18 make the point clear. To show two aspects of his ministry, Jesus actually makes two applications of the illustration he has used.

First of all he uses the reference to the door (vss. 1-3) and describes himself as "the door of the sheep" (vs. 7; see also vs. 9). To get into the proper place of safety and refuge, one must enter the right door. Jesus is the door through which believers enter into life with the Father (compare 7:13-14); he is "the new and living way" of access to God (Heb. 10:20; see also Eph. 2:18).

False leaders claiming to be God's Messiah had preceded him
(vs. 8). The reference was not to the Old Testament prophets
and writers, who were faithful to God and pointed forward to
Christ; it was rather to leaders in more recent times who had
falsely claimed to fulfill the promise that God would send his
Messiah to Israel. The true Jews had not accepted these false
leaders but had recognized them as "thieves and robbers" who
would harm the sheep of God. It is only through Jesus that men
find God, are saved, are kept safely, and find their needs met
(vs. 9). For the aim of Jesus is not like that of thieves, who
only want to steal and destroy; he came to give full and abundant
life to all who come to the Father through him (vs. 10).

So it is clear that it is not enough to call Jesus "the door."
He is the living "way" to life (14:6); he actively cares for his
people. Therefore he makes a fuller statement of his work when
he calls himself "the good shepherd" (vss. 11, 14). His love for
his sheep and his faithfulness in caring for them go so far that he
even gives his life for them; the Cross is included in the Good
Shepherd's care for his sheep. In this complete dedication and
sacrificial ministry Jesus is entirely different from a "hireling,"
a leader who thinks only of his own interests and the pay that he
gets for his work. When such a hireling sees that a wolf—that is,
any danger—is approaching, he thinks not of protecting and saving
the sheep but only of acting for his own safety; he flees for his
life and lets the wolf seize and tear the sheep (vss. 12-13). He
lacks the shepherd's heart which Jesus has. Jesus knows his own
sheep; as verse 3 has said, he knows each one by name, and they
know and trust him (vs. 14). This relation between Jesus and
his followers is comparable even to the mutual knowledge and
trust that exists between Jesus and God the Father (vs. 15).
There is complete knowledge and trust between himself and his
followers, and his care for them is so complete that he lays down
his life for his sheep. Indeed, it is his faithfulness and dedication—
not that of his followers—which explains the close mutual tie
between him and them.

In verses 7-15 Jesus has centered attention on his relation to
those in Israel who respond to him in faith. But in verse 16 he
opens up a broader view. He has other sheep, outside the Jewish
circle, who must be brought to know him as their Shepherd. During his ministry Jesus did not extend his ministry to Gentiles.
Rarely did he speak with them or do anything for them; he was

sent to the lost sheep of the house of Israel (Matt. 15:24); even Paul, the great Apostle to the Gentiles, said that the gospel was sent "to the Jew first" (Rom. 1:16). But Jesus looked to a day when other peoples would be included in the one flock of which he would be the one Shepherd (3:16; Matt. 8:11; 24:14; 28:19).

The death of the Shepherd for his flock is not forced upon him; he voluntarily accepts it. Such complete dedication to his people explains the love which the Father has for him (vs. 17). The Father has given him the charge to save his people by suffering and resurrection, and the Son willingly gives his life and takes it back again in glory (vs. 18). Because he thus uses his power to carry out the Father's saving will, the Father loves him and the complete harmony between Father and Son continues (vs. 30).

The teaching of Jesus continually forces men to decide for or against him; it causes a division between those who believe and those who reject him. In verse 19 the Jews again divided. Some thought he was demented; instead of seeing in his teaching and acts the good work of the Holy Spirit, as 1:32 would suggest, they explained his allegedly unbalanced state by the presence of a demon in him, and impatiently told the others not to listen to so demon-possessed a man (vs. 20). But the others, while not declaring their faith in Jesus, pointed out that this teaching was sane and solid truth and obviously not demon-inspired (vs. 21); moreover, a demon could not do such good works as the healing of the man born blind (9:1-7; in Matthew 12:22-32, however, the Pharisees actually do explain Jesus' healings in this way). Such true teaching, such helpful deeds—what but the power of God could explain such work by Jesus?

Jesus at the Feast of Dedication (10:22-39)

The Feast of Dedication, held on the twenty-fifth of the month Chislev (about our Christmas time), celebrated the rededication of the Temple by Judas Maccabaeus in 164 B.C. The Syrian ruler Antiochus Epiphanes had desecrated and despoiled the Temple, but after a bitter struggle the Jews had got it back and cleansed and rededicated it. At that winter time, with Jerusalem nearly 2600 feet above sea level, it was cold, and Jesus, who apparently had been in Jerusalem since the fall Feast of Tabernacles (7:2, 10, 14), was walking in the sheltered portico of Solomon, on the east side of the outer court of the Temple (vss. 22-23).

The hostile leaders of the Jews felt that Jesus had not come out

clearly with his claim, so they gathered around him, to keep him
there until he answered, and demanded that he tell them plainly
whether he claimed to be the Christ whom the Jews expected (vs.
24). He said that he had already told them (vs. 25). So far in
this Gospel he had spoken no such explicit claim to the Jews as he
did to the Samaritan woman (4:26), but he had repeatedly implied that he was that unique leader sent by God. And, as 5:36
has said, the works he had done made clear that he deserved their
faith; these works were a witness that men of good will would
find convincing. Why, then, did so many refuse to believe? "Because you do not belong to my sheep" (vs. 26). Without denying
that those who refused him were guilty and to be condemned,
Jesus traced this rejection to the wisdom and determination of
God, under whose care and control all men live (compare 8:47).
Those whom the Father has given him as his sheep hear, know,
and follow him, and he keeps them safe and gives them eternal
life now and in the age to come (vss. 27-28). The Father is
greater than all possible enemies of his sheep (vs. 29). Jesus and
the Father are one in purpose and in love for the sheep (vs. 30);
no one can thwart or defeat the Father's saving purpose, which
Jesus actively shares.

The claim of Jesus to be one with the Father seemed blasphemous to his Jewish critics. They got stones and prepared to
stone him for blasphemy (vs. 31). Jesus bitingly asked for which
of his good works they intended to stone him (vs. 32). They
disregarded the point that he had been doing good, as one truly
sent of God would do, and fixed upon his claim to oneness with
God, by which they understood that he was making himself God
or identifying himself with God (vs. 33). Jesus replied with a
Scripture reference that would carry point for Jews (vs. 34).
Psalm 82:6 is here called the Law; in a broad sense the entire
Scripture, and not just the five books of Moses, was thought of
by Jews as the Law of God. In Psalm 82:6, Jesus said, God spoke
to the Israelites and called them "gods." No Jew would admit
that the Scripture could be "broken", or discarded as untrue. So
God called Israelites gods (vs. 35). How much more, Jesus said
(vs. 36), could the unique Son, consecrated and sent into the
world by the Father, be called—he does not say "God," but—
"the Son of God"! As the words "my Father" in verse 37 indicate, Jesus did claim to be the Son of God in a special and unparalleled sense, and he was aware, as verse 38 indicates, that he

lived in a unique relation of oneness with the Father. He did not want to be accepted as a political and nationalistic Messiah, but if they would face the fact that the Christ is the Son of God in this unique sense of oneness with the Father (20:31), they could see that he did claim to be the Christ.

Jesus' hearers understood that he was claiming more than they would admit, more than they considered it proper for any man to claim, so they wanted to arrest him, but he escaped (vs. 39). Until his "hour" came—that is, his time to die—they could not seize and kill him.

The Ministry East of Jordan (10:40-42)

The public ministry of Jesus was practically ended. This Gospel reports no more extended preaching in Jerusalem. But Jesus went east, across the Jordan River, to Bethany on the east bank, where John the Baptist had formerly preached and baptized (vs. 40; compare 1:28), and there many came to see and hear him. They recalled that John himself had done no sign or miracle; he had preached about the coming of the Greater One who was to follow him. The crowds testified that Jesus fulfilled this promise. It is implied that Jesus did there "signs" which showed that he had divine power in a way that John did not (vs. 41). The response was more favorable than it had been in Jerusalem; many believed in him (vs. 42).

How long Jesus was in this region is not said, but since verses 22-39 were dated late in December, and the next Jewish feast mentioned is the spring Passover (11:55), the stay at Bethany beyond Jordan apparently lasted only a few weeks. Between that December feast and the Passover in March or April there occurred not only the stay at Bethany east of Jordan but also the return to Judea to raise Lazarus (11:7, 17) and the stay, probably quite brief, at Ephraim (11:54).

Jesus the Resurrection and the Life (11:1-44)

Lazarus has not been mentioned before in this Gospel, nor is he mentioned in the other Gospels. (The Lazarus in the parable of Luke 16:19-31 is not the same man.) Mary and Martha appear in Luke 10:38-42 as residents of a village which seems to be located on the border between Galilee and Samaria (Luke 9:51; 17:11). Luke groups much of his material in a travel narrative which pictures Jesus going from Galilee to Jerusalem (9:51—

19:44); in all probability he did not know the exact place where
some incidents occurred and simply placed them in a convenient
position in his story. So Luke may not have known that Mary and
Martha lived with their brother Lazarus at Bethany (vs. 1), just
east of Jerusalem on the southeast slope of the Mount of Olives.
Mary is identified as the one who anointed the Lord Jesus (vs.
2). This event is not reported until 12:1-8, but its mention here
prepares the reader for what is coming. Perhaps Mary is mentioned in this special way because she was widely known in the
Church for this anointing (Mark 14:9). Chapter 11 assumes that
Lazarus and his two sisters were disciples.

When Lazarus fell sick, the sisters sent word to Jesus (vs. 3).
He was at Bethany beyond Jordan (10:40; see 1:28). They did
not ask him to come; they took it for granted that when he heard
that Lazarus was sick he would come and would be able to heal
his friend, for they knew that Jesus loved Lazarus. The repeated
reference to this love in verses 3, 5, 11, and 36 makes it clear that
Jesus had a special affection for Lazarus. He is the only man
named in the entire Gospel for whom Jesus is said to have had
a personal love. Since Jesus thus loved Lazarus, the sisters were
confident that he would not delay to come.

But as the Fourth Gospel repeatedly emphasizes, Jesus never
let others tell him what to do. Even when he did what others
asked, he first indicated his independence, and on occasion even
delayed a little, as he did here (vs. 6). This may seem heartless
to us, but it is the way the writer brings out the fact that the
Son of God acted on his own initiative and followed the will of
God. Verse 4 gives another reason for delay. The sickness, Jesus
said, would not result in (final, spiritual) death, but would
promote the glory of God and of his Son. It would show the
presence and power of God in Jesus as he dealt with the physical
death of Lazarus; it would bring praise and honor both to the
Father and to the Son when God's power exercised by Jesus
proved master even over death.

Jesus loved the two sisters as well as their brother (vs. 5).
But they had not learned that his love and power could reach
beyond physical death; they did not understand how complete
was the gift of life he could give. So he stayed two days at
Bethany beyond Jordan after hearing that Lazarus was sick (vs.
6). From verses 17 and 39 ("four days") it seems that the messenger took one day to reach Jesus; Jesus then waited two days,

and on the fourth day he journeyed with his disciples to Bethany near Jerusalem.

After the two days, Jesus summoned his disciples to go with him back to Judea. (Bethany beyond Jordan was not in Judea but in Perea. It was governed by Herod Antipas.) The disciples objected (vs. 8), even though he was their Teacher and Master ("Rabbi"). The hostile Jews had recently tried to stone him in Jerusalem (10:31); to return would invite renewed efforts to kill him (and perhaps them!). Jesus recalled that there are only twelve hours in the day (vs. 9); that is, the time allotted for his ministry was limited, and he must carry out each stage of his ministry at the appointed time and without regard to danger. Just as a man who walks by the light of the sun does not stumble (vs. 9), so Jesus would suffer no real defeat by doing the will of his Father. The light of his leading from the Father told him that he must go to the home of his friends, and he would be walking in darkness if he did not follow that light (vs. 10). He had to go back; his return was a part of his ministry.

Then, in one of the ambiguous statements characteristic of this Gospel, Jesus said that Lazarus had fallen asleep and he must go and waken him (vs. 11). The disciples took this to mean that the crisis of the illness was past; not knowing that Lazarus had died, they thought that Jesus meant the sleep of a man on the way to recovery (vs. 12). Jesus, with his deeper knowledge, knew that Lazarus had died (vs. 13). He told them so (vs. 14), and added that his absence when Lazarus died would have a good result for the disciples. Seeing his power to give life would give them new reason to believe; it would lead them to a fuller, deeper faith (vs. 15). They did not understand this. Thomas, the chronically pessimistic disciple, apparently expressed the attitude of the group. He loyally urged that they all go with Jesus but darkly expected that they, too, would die (vs. 16). The renewed attempt on Jesus' life (10:31) would succeed and the Jewish wrath would also bring death to his disciples. The name "Thomas" (Hebrew in origin) means "Twin"; Thomas was also called "Didymus," the Greek word for Twin. Who his twin brother or sister was we do not know.

When Jesus reached Bethany, Lazarus had been dead and buried for four days (vs. 17; compare vs. 39); burial followed death rather quickly. This would mean that Lazarus died almost at once after the messenger left Bethany. Bethany was not quite two miles from Jerusalem. (The Greek in verse 18 says "fifteen stadia"; a "stade" was 600 Greek feet.) So it was natural that Jerusalem Jews who knew the sisters had come to console them (vs. 19). Martha, probably the older of the sisters and the active head of the home, was the first to be told that Jesus was approaching (vs. 20), and she went to the edge of the village to meet him (vs. 30), while Mary stayed in the house with the guests.

Martha at once said what the sisters must have said or thought often in the last four days: had Jesus been present, he would have been able to heal Lazarus and prevent his death; he would have used his power to help his friend (vs. 21). She still vaguely believed that whatever Jesus saw could be done would be done by God's gift and working (vs. 22), but she had no particular solution in mind. Jesus assured her that her brother would rise again (vs. 23). Taking this to mean that Lazarus would rise at the last day, when all rise from the dead, she agreed (vs. 24). Probably she had heard the same thing from friends in the last four days, and had agreed with them, but it seemed a poor substitute for having Lazarus alive. She failed to see that in Jesus the fact of resurrection and the gift of life were present before her.

Jesus is the Resurrection and the Life; he can raise the dead and he gives life that death cannot touch. This double gift is available to those who believe. Even if a believer dies, Jesus will raise him at the last day (and of that Lazarus is to become an acted parable); and even physical death will not really harm the believer, for the life that Jesus gives to those who believe in him is a gift that physical death cannot take away or damage (vss. 25-26). Martha said that she believed this; perhaps she did not really and deeply know the immediate meaning and promise of what he said, but she knew essentially who Jesus was, for she identified him as "the Christ, the Son of God" (vs. 27), and she is the only person in this Gospel to make this exact confession which the Gospel was written to promote (20:31). He had come into the world as the promised Christ of Israel, and he was more than a merely human leader, for he was the Son of God in whom the presence and power of God were uniquely incarnate to help men.

Jesus evidently asked to see Mary, and Martha tried to tell her, without attracting the attention of the guests, that Jesus wanted to see her (vs. 28). Her quick movement when she heard this showed how much she had wanted Jesus to come (vs. 29), but it also alerted the guests, and they followed her to the place where Jesus waited, just outside of Bethany (vs. 30); they thought she was going to the tomb of Lazarus to weep over his death (vs. 31). Mary repeated the rather despairing and wistful lament of the sisters: if Jesus had only been there he could and would have kept Lazarus from dying (vs. 32). But she said no more. Her actions—here in falling at Jesus' feet, and later in anointing them in preparation for his impending death and burial—showed her deep grief, her strong loyalty to Jesus, and, it is implied, her understanding of what lay ahead for Jesus.

When Jesus saw the grief of Mary and of the Jews with her, it moved him to delay no longer what he had come to do (vs. 33). He asked where the body was (vs. 34), and wept as they started with him to the tomb (vs. 35).

The Jews who had come to comfort the sisters saw that Jesus' weeping showed his great love for Lazarus (vs. 36). In this Gospel, Lazarus is the only man named of whom it is said that Jesus loved him (see vss. 3, 5, 11, 36); the natural inference, as the Introduction points out, is that Lazarus was "the disciple whom Jesus loved" (see 13:23; 19:26-27; 20:2-10; 21:7, 20-24). But not all of the Jews present were sympathetic with Jesus. Some were critical (vs. 37). Jesus had opened the eyes of the blind (9:1-7); why did he not keep his own friend from dying? The writer suggests Jesus' answer to such a question in 11:15, 25-26, 40.

The tomb, like many found in Palestine, was a cave, closed by a stone which covered the entrance (vs. 38). Jesus asked that the stone be taken away from the entrance so that the dead man, when raised, could come out (vs. 39). Martha protested, recalling that the body had lain there four days and must have begun to decay. She thus showed that she did not understand Jesus' purpose or think that he could do what he intended. He reminded her that he had promised (in veiled form in verse 25) that if she believed she would see the glory of God (vs. 40); only expectant believers could thus see God's power present and active in Jesus to achieve his divine purpose. The family and friends then complied with Jesus' command; the stone was taken away (vs. 41a).

The prayer that Jesus offered was unusual (vss. 41b-42). He did not ask the Father to hear him and give him power to raise

Lazarus; he thanked the Father for having already heard him.
This probably means that Jesus had already prayed, and knew
that his prayer was answered and that Lazarus was being raised
or would now be raised. As the Son, Jesus had received from the
Father the power to give life (5:21, 26), and he knew that this
prayer was certainly granted. He made this public prayer, not
just for show, but so that all onlookers might know of his previous prayer and its answer, and might be led, once they saw by
Lazarus' resurrection that Jesus' prayer and obedience had been
recognized and honored by the Father, to believe that the Father
had sent him. Then with a loud, authoritative voice he commanded
Lazarus to come out of the tomb (vs. 43). The dead man—that
is, the man who had been dead—came out, his movements im-
peded by the bandages and headcloth in which he had been
wrapped when prepared for burial. Jesus commanded those
standing by to remove the bandages and headcloth and let
Lazarus return to his home and normal life (vs. 44).

This miracle showed that Jesus is the Resurrection and the
Life (vs. 25), able to raise the dead and to give them life. It was
a sign to those of faith that the Son of God not only gives life
to all at creation and sustains life in all men of every generation
(1:3-4, 9) but also redeems men from sin now (1:29) and will
raise them from the dead at the last day. To all who believe, he
gives eternal life now and in the age to come. Thus this climactic
miracle of Jesus' ministry teaches dramatically the truth which
the Gospel was written to enforce: those who believe in Jesus
as the Christ, the Son of God, receive through him the gift of
eternal life (20:31).

The Ministry Ended, Jesus Faces the Cross (11:45—12:50)

Many of the Jews present with Mary and Martha at the tomb
believed in Jesus (vs. 45); they saw the glory of God revealed
in this mighty act he had done (see vs. 40). But others told the
Pharisees in Jerusalem "what Jesus had done" (vs. 46). Did they
do this out of hostility to Jesus? Or did they think that the religious leaders should recognize Jesus' authority? We are not told.

The "chief priests and the Pharisees," that is, the Jewish
Sanhedrin, the highest council and court of the Jews, met to
consider what to do (vs. 47). They saw in Jesus' action a claim
and a challenge to them. This was but one of "many signs" which
Jesus had done. If he were allowed to continue his ministry, the

rulers anticipated that he would win the Jewish people, and thus would displace them from their leadership of that people. They also feared what the Romans might do. The Romans were in control of Palestine but allowed considerable freedom to the Jews and the Jewish leaders as long as the people were quiet and obedient to Rome. But if the rise of Jesus to power led to public disturbance, the Romans would doubtless step in, destroy Jerusalem and the Temple, and take away even the partial freedom that the Jews still had (vs. 48).

Caiaphas had a plan to prevent this. He was high priest that year (vs. 49); in fact, he was high priest from A.D. 18 to 36, but the Gospel mentions "that year" as especially important because it was the year in which the Jewish leaders took action to have Jesus executed. Caiaphas callously said that if one man—he meant Jesus, of course—makes a disturbance, it is better to kill him than to let the situation get out of hand and bring ruin to the entire Jewish people. He spoke cynically: let one man die for the people (vs. 50). But the Christian writer saw in this an unconscious and unintended Christian truth, that Jesus did in fact die for all the Jews and for all the other sheep of his flock scattered abroad in the world (vss. 51-52; see 10:16). Verse 51 says that Caiaphas, as the high priest and so the official leader of God's people, spoke as a prophet; that is, he was used by God to state the meaning of Jesus' death, but he did not know he was doing so.

Did the Church and the Gospel writer have any real way of knowing what went on in secret meetings of the Sanhedrin? Nicodemus and others of "the authorities" in the Sanhedrin were sympathetic to the gospel and could have told what happened in such secret meetings (3:1; 12:42).

The conclusion of this secret meeting was the determination to act promptly to put Jesus to death (vs. 53). Thus in this Gospel what led to the final decision to act at once to kill Jesus was not, as in the other Gospels, the cleansing of the Temple (see John 2:13-22), but was rather the resurrection of Lazarus and the popular favor which that "sign" brought to Jesus.

Verses 45-53 are in a sense the beginning of the Passion story; they tell of the final decision to act at once to get Jesus put to death. But the leaders did not succeed at once in their purpose. Jesus broke off his public ministry in Jerusalem, and went to Ephraim, a town about fourteen miles north by northeast of

Jerusalem (vs. 54). There he stayed until six days before the
Passover (12:1).

Verse 55 implies that the stay at Ephraim was short; Passover
time was close at hand. Great numbers of Jews went to Jerusalem
for the Passover celebration, at which the Passover Supper recalled the deliverance of Israel from Egypt and raised hopes that
God would again deliver his people. To observe the feast the
Jews had to be properly purified in accordance with Jewish ceremonial law, so they planned to reach Jerusalem a few days early
to carry out the purifying rites and complete the plans for the
Passover.

Groups gathered in the Temple courts and quietly discussed
among themselves whether Jesus would have the courage to come
to the feast (vs. 56). It was known that the Sanhedrin ("the chief
priests and the Pharisees") had ordered that anyone who knew
where Jesus was should give them the information. They wanted
to arrest him and get rid of him permanently (vs. 57). They did
not realize that his death would bring him glory and would give
world outreach to his movement.

The Passover meal was prepared on the fourteenth day of the
month of Nisan and eaten on the fifteenth day, which began at
sundown. Jesus was crucified on Friday (19:31, 42), according
to this Gospel, and as 18:28 indicates, the meal eaten by Jesus
on Thursday evening was not the Passover Supper. That was still
to be eaten on Friday evening (when, according to Jewish reck-
oning, the Sabbath had begun). So "six days before the Passover"
(vs. 1) was six days before that Sabbath; it was the preceding
Sunday. On that day Jesus arrived at Bethany (12:1) from
Ephraim (11:54). (The other Gospels date the Passover on
Thursday evening, but the Gospel of John may well be right in its
dating.)

The only Bethany people mentioned by name in this Gospel are
Lazarus, Martha, and Mary. This implies that Jesus stayed at
their home, and that the supper (vs. 2) was served there; the
fact that Martha served it confirms this. Lazarus of course was
present, an object of attention as the man whom Jesus had raised
from the dead. But at that supper in Bethany, Mary was the center of interest (vs. 3). As already mentioned in 11:2, she
"anointed the Lord with ointment." The ointment was costly.
Verse 5 means that its worth equaled an unskilled laborer's wages
for three hundred days; a denarius was a day laborer's pay for

one day's work. Mary had prepared a plentiful supply; a "pound," or Roman *libra*, was about twelve ounces. It was genuine nard, an ointment or perfume (vs. 3 mentions its pervasive fragrance) made from the root of the nard plant. With it Mary anointed Jesus' feet, then wiped the feet with her loosened hair.

In Mark 14:3 (compare Matt. 26:7) an unnamed woman broke a jar of ointment and poured all of the contents on Jesus' head. In Luke 7:37-38 a sinful woman's tears fell on his feet; she wiped his feet with her loosened hair, and anointed them with ointment. The stories in John and Luke are most alike. Do they refer to the same woman? Was the sinful woman Mary of Bethany? In John there is no hint that Mary was a penitent sinner, unless it is the fact of her loosened hair. The shadow of the impending Cross is here the implied reason she anointed Jesus' feet. Jesus was reclining on a couch to eat. Mary could easily approach his feet as he lay with his head at the edge of the table.

Judas Iscariot objected to her act. Verse 4 sadly recalls that he was a disciple; a disciple—yet about to betray his Lord. His objection sounded reasonable; Jesus had sympathy for the poor and condemned wasteful luxury. To use three hundred days' wages for one anointing—even the anointing of God's Anointed One, Messiah, Christ—could seem reckless extravagance, contrary to Jesus' teaching and way of life. Why not give the money to the poor? (vs. 5). This Gospel alone adds another point: Judas had no real care for the poor; he was a thief; he kept taking money from the money box which he carried as treasurer of the group (vs. 6). Greed, not sacrificial kindness, was back of his protest.

What does verse 7 say that Jesus replied to Judas? The Greek words may mean: "Let her alone; let her keep the ointment and use it on the day of my burial." But she had already used at least part of it. Perhaps the reason she needed to wipe Jesus' feet after anointing them was that she had poured it on his feet so lavishly. So the meaning of verses 7-8 may be: "Let her alone; let her perform this act now and so, by anticipation, prepare my body for the burial which so soon will come. She need not save the ointment; it is proper for her to use it in this way. If you are really concerned for the poor, you will have daily opportunities to help them; they are always present, needing help. But this is a special occasion: the time to show lovingkindness to me is almost past; I am soon to die."

The great crowd present in Jerusalem for the Passover Feast

(see 11:55) came to Bethany to see both Jesus and Lazarus (vs. 9). We are not to suppose that every Passover pilgrim did this; what the Gospel describes is the general popular interest in Jesus. Great as was their interest in Jesus, however, their interest in Lazarus, a man whom Jesus had raised from the dead, was, for the time at least, equally great. This led "the chief priests"—probably this means the Sanhedrin—to plan for the death not only of Jesus (11:53) but also of Lazarus (vs. 10). Lazarus as "Exhibit A" was impressing many people with Jesus' divine power and leading them to believe in Jesus (vs. 11). So the leaders decided to put Lazarus to death before the tide of faith in Jesus became too strong to oppose. Is this plan a clue to what became of Lazarus? Does it explain why we hear nothing of him in the story of the Apostolic Age? It was natural for the chief priests to be especially hostile to Lazarus. They, as Sadducees, did not believe in the resurrection (Acts 23:8) and so would oppose any teaching or stories that seemed to support that doctrine. Probably they explained the story of the resurrection of Lazarus as a fraud.

The next day, which, as we must infer from verse 1, was Monday, five days before the Passover, Jesus made a triumphal entry into Jerusalem amid great enthusiasm. Two crowds were involved. One (vs. 12) was the crowd of worshipers who had come to Jerusalem early to purify themselves and so be ready to observe the Passover according to Jewish rules (11:55). When they heard the excited report that Jesus was approaching Jerusalem, they went out to meet him with branches of palm trees. How they could get palm branches at Jerusalem at that time of year we do not know. They were a regular feature of the observance of the Feast of Tabernacles in the fall; here they were used in a spontaneous way to give Jesus special honor (vs. 13); they were not a regular part of the Passover celebration, and in any case the Passover, according to this Gospel, had not yet come (18:28).

Waving palm branches, the people went out the eastern city gate to meet Jesus as he rounded the southern slope of the Mount of Olives and approached Jerusalem. Their cry on meeting him echoed Psalm 118:25-26. "Hosanna," a word of Hebrew origin meaning literally "Save now," is used here as a shout of welcome and tribute to Jesus and praise to God. The welcoming words that follow describe Jesus as sent of God: he comes in the name of the Lord and as the expected King of Israel, that is, as God's promised Messiah.

This latter idea of the coming King occurs also in the other Scripture passage cited. Jesus found a young ass and rode it into the city (vs. 14; where he found it, or whether he sent his disciples to get it, as the other three Gospels report, this Gospel does not say). This recalls to the Gospel writer Zechariah 9:9, where the "daughter of Zion" (the people of the city of Jerusalem) are told that their king or anointed leader is coming, mounted not on a horse that might carry a great warrior but on an ass's colt; and so, in a way, the act symbolizes the peaceful spirit of the true Messianic King of Israel (vs. 15). In this acted parable Jesus expressed the spirit of his life and ministry; he pointed to the Cross rather than to war and conquest as the spirit and symbol of his work for men. But as in 2:22, the writer says that this meaning of the event did not become clear to Jesus' followers until after he had died, risen, and so been glorified. Then, as they looked back on his acts, they noted how the Scriptures pointed forward to his work (vs. 16).

The crowd from Jerusalem was met not only by Jesus but also by the crowd that accompanied Jesus from Bethany (vs. 17). Some of the latter group could tell interested listeners how Jesus raised Lazarus from the dead. These eyewitnesses received an eager hearing; that very resurrection report had caused many to go out to meet Jesus (vs. 18). Everyone, it seemed, was being swept into acceptance of Jesus as sent of God. The Pharisees, present as unconvinced but alert spectators, told each other sourly that they were getting nowhere with their campaign against Jesus; with exaggeration they said that the world had gone after him (vs. 19). But a very few days would show that a volatile crowd, whose faith was not based on true understanding, could not stand up against a numerically small but determined and crafty opposition.

To the Gospel writer the next event was of immense significance. Some "Greeks"—that is, Gentiles who were interested in the Jewish faith and had come to worship in Jerusalem at Passover time (vs. 20)—came to Philip, who had a Greek name and probably spoke Greek. They asked to see Jesus (vs. 21). Philip knew that Jesus had not ministered to Gentiles; puzzled about what to do, he asked help of his fellow townsman Andrew (1:44). The two of them reported the request to Jesus (vs. 22). To Jesus this was a decisive event. He was aware that his mission had a world outreach (10:16; see 3:16; 4:42; 8:12); both the Jewish roots (4:22) and the world scope of the gospel are clear in this

Gospel. The coming of the Greeks symbolized the future world-
wide spread of the Christian witness. But it meant something else.
To Jesus it was the clue that now the hour of his death was at
hand (vs. 23); the hour had come for him to be glorified, by his
willing suffering as the Lamb of God (1:29). He would be exalted to the Father by being lifted up on the cross.

This is the principle of fruitful spiritual life. Life selfishly preserved and protected is barren; only life given in sacrifice and
death yields the harvest. This is the way it is in the harvest of
grain; only as the seed dies and decays can it spring up in new
and fruitful life (vs. 24). To love one's life, to think always of
physical safety and personal advantage, is to lose real life; it keeps
one from fellowship with God and from service to his purpose.
To hate one's life, to serve God at the cost of personal privilege
or even of physical life, is to keep one's real life and win, through
sacrifice of selfish interest, eternal life in blessed fellowship with
God and Christ (vs. 25). For this way of the Cross, this losing of
one's life to find it, is not for Jesus alone. It is for all who will
follow Jesus (vs. 26). They must live in his spirit; then they will
suffer with their Lord, and will know the joy, the victory, the
blessing, and the glory which came to Jesus through being "faithful unto death" (Rev. 2:10).

Verses 27-28 are this Gospel's nearest parallel to Jesus' inner
struggle at Gethsemane as reported in the other Gospels (compare, for example, Mark 14:33-36). The soul of Jesus was troubled as he faced his imminent death. Should he ask God to save
him from this hour of suffering? No, he could not ask that; the
purpose of his coming was to be fulfilled precisely in this hour
of suffering on the cross. So he accepted the cross, and asked the
Father to glorify the Father's name, that is, to bring praise to
the Father as he is made known by this suffering of his Son on
the cross.

The voice from heaven, the voice of the Father, replied that he
had already glorified his name, especially in the sending and the
ministry of the Son, and he promised to glorify it again by exalting his Son through crucifixion. The voice was a way of express-
ing to the Gospel reader the divine approval of Jesus' ministry
and impending death. The bystanders, it is said, did not understand this heavenly voice (vs. 29). Some thought it a clap of thun-
der; others thought it the voice of an angel; but no one, it appears,
clearly understood it. Yet it came, Jesus said, to give divine ap-

proval to his life and especially to his words in verses 23-28. It was given to help his hearers and not to reassure Jesus, who did not need such help.

Jesus had said that the hour for his death had come (vs. 23); verse 31 describes it as the hour of judgment on the hostile world, the hour when the Devil, the apparently powerful but really doomed ruler of that hostile realm, was to be cast out of his supposed kingdom. Through the Cross the kingdom of this world was to become the Kingdom of the Lord and of his Christ (Rev. 11:15). Jesus, lifted up from the earth on the cross and so exalted to honor with the Father, was to draw all men to himself (vs. 32). The gospel is for the world.

The Greeks of verse 20 have been lost from view; we are not even told whether they got to see Jesus. The occasion is used to announce Jesus' Passion and its world-wide benefits. For in speaking of being lifted up from the earth Jesus referred to his death (vs. 33) and its attendant glory. He would be exalted, lifted up to the Father, not in spite of or after being lifted up on the cross, but precisely through being lifted up on the cross.

Jesus' hearers sensed that he was speaking of his death. They knew of and perhaps had shared in the shouts that Jesus was the promised Christ (vss. 13, 15). But they had expected the Christ, when he came, to remain with them forever, not subject to defeat or death (vs. 34). Being lifted up on the cross did not fit their ideas of the Messiah. "Who is this Son of man" if he must thus be exalted by being crucified?

Jesus did not answer their question directly. He told his hearers what they needed to do. He was and is the Light (1:4; 8:12). Just as a man must walk about and do his work while he has the light of the sun or he will stumble over things in the dark, so his hearers should walk in the Light (vss. 35-36a); they should believe in him as the Light of life so that they might become sons of light who reflect that light to others (Matt. 5:16).

It has been suggested that verses 36b-43 should follow 44-50. Then verses 44-50, which summarize Jesus' message, would follow well after 36a, and verses 36b-43 would state well the largely negative response to his public ministry. In some ways this would be a good order, but no manuscripts support it. Moreover, this Gospel is not concerned to present a logical and closely knit narrative, and it often returns to repeat an idea given earlier. Why was the order ever changed, if verses 44-50 once preceded verses

36b-43? It is better to leave the two sections in the order which
the Greek texts and English translations present.

In verse 36b, as in 8:59, Jesus hid himself from the crowd with
which he had been talking (vs. 34). Where he went is not said;
the other Gospels suggest Bethany, on the southeastern slope of
the Mount of Olives (compare Mark 11:11, 19; 14:3). Verses
37-41 sum up the generally unbelieving response of the Jews.
Jesus had done many signs among them that pointed to God's
presence and power in him. But they did not believe in him (vs.
37). This did not shake the faith of the Gospel writer or the
Church, for the Old Testament had indicated that it would happen. Isaiah 53:1 had said that unbelief would meet the Servant
of God as he brought to men God's words ("report") and deeds
(indicated by "the arm of the LORD"); Jesus as the Suffering
Servant had experienced precisely the unbelief and rejection
which Scripture had anticipated (vs. 38).

Indeed, the writer adds an even stronger statement. The hostile
Jews could not believe; a divinely predestined blindness and deafness had struck Israel, just as Isaiah 6:10 had indicated it would
(vss. 39-40). This does not mean that God had blinded and
deafened Israel in spite of their previous good life or sincere
longing to hear and do God's will; it means that this divinely
effected penal blindness and deafness had an expression and secondary basis in their persistently rebellious attitude, their stubborn hostility to the gospel, and their consistent disobedience to
God. The prior sovereign working of God and the responsible,
guilty actions of these men were both real facts. They had turned
from the very Person and message that offered the cure for their
spiritual sickness. Isaiah 6:10 was reporting how God had described in ironical words the anticipated failure of the prophet's
own ministry. The Gospel writer found that in the last analysis
Isaiah 6:10 spoke of Jesus and of the divine glory which faith
could discern in his rejected ministry.

Here again this Gospel makes first an absolute statement: "they
did not believe in him" (vs. 37), and later adds a qualification:
many of the leaders—but still a minority—did believe in him (vs.
42). Why then did not these believers, the Sanhedrin members
who recognized that Jesus was the Christ, the Son of God, say so
openly and block the movement to execute Jesus? Nicodemus
came to Jesus by night (3:1-2), mildly defended Jesus' right to a
fair hearing (7:50-51), and helped to bury Jesus in a costly way

(19:39). Joseph of Arimathea, who perhaps was a Sanhedrin member (19:38), took the initiative in burying Jesus. But neither these men nor any other leading Jew openly opposed the plan to kill Jesus. Why? "For fear of the Pharisees" (the most influential Jewish leaders)—for fear they would be put out of the synagogue, the special place of influence of the Pharisees. They preferred honor from men more than the honor God gives to those who truly believe and openly witness to Christ (vs. 43). A withering condemnation! They had a kind of faith, but it was a faith that put God's will second. For the Gospel writer, God must not be put second; such a faith was not adequate for salvation.

Verses 44-50 give no new message; they summarize Jesus' previous teaching. To believe in Jesus is to believe in the Father who sent him (vs. 44). To see Jesus, to discern who he is and what he offers and requires, is to see the Father who sent him (vs. 45). Jesus came as light: "In him was life, and the life was the light of men" (1:4); he was and is "the light of the world" (8:12); he came to bring light so that whoever believes in him may not remain in the spiritual and moral darkness due to sin and separation from God (vs. 46). It is possible to reject Jesus' gracious offer. To hear his words is not enough; to enter into light and find life one must keep them, remember and obey them. Many refuse to do that. These Jesus does not judge directly (vs. 47); his great aim in coming into human life was not to judge and condemn anyone (3:17-18; compare 9:39) but to save the world from its moral darkness. A day of final judgment is coming, and on that day the teaching of Jesus will bring every unbeliever under judgment (vs. 48).

It is not surprising that Jesus' words have such crucial importance and eternal consequences. He did not speak merely as a human authority; the Father who sent him told him what to say (vss. 49-50), and he was careful to speak just what the Father sent him to speak (17:8; see Deut. 18:18). The divine commandment, accepted in faith and obeyed in life, gives eternal life. The responsive, obedient believer is in the right relation with the Father and the Son, and that is the very essence of eternal life (17:3).

JESUS' FINAL MINISTRY TO HIS FAITHFUL FOLLOWERS
John 13:1—17:26

The Footwashing Teaches Mutual Humble Love (13:1-38)

Chapters 11 and 12 of the Gospel prepare for the story of Jesus' death. The resurrection of Lazarus presents the theme of life through resurrection; Jesus is the Resurrection and the Life (11:25). The anointing at Bethany (12:1-8) points on to Jesus' burial; the triumphal entry is his final offer to the Jerusalem people and their leaders (12:12-19); the desire of the Greeks to see him is the clue that his hour to suffer and thereby to give life to the world has come (12:20-23). Now, in chapter 13, the Last Supper brings the story close to the actual hour of the Cross.

Jesus Washes the Feet of His Disciples (13:1-11)

In this Gospel the Last Supper is eaten on the evening before the Passover (13:1; 18:28; 19:14), rather than on the Passover evening as in the other Gospels. Jesus knew what was impending (vss. 1, 3, 11, 18); nothing surprised or dismayed him. Throughout his ministry he had loved "his own," his followers who were in the world. He now must leave them in the world, and he performed one last act of love and service to teach them a much needed lesson. He washed the disciples' feet, not at the beginning of supper as a host might do in courtesy, but during supper, because the disciples needed a lesson which a symbolic act could teach. His special concern in this act was not with Judas but with the others. He knew that Judas would betray him (6:70-71); this Satanic purpose was already in Judas' heart, waiting for an opportunity (vs. 2), but his final decision to act had not yet been made (see vs. 27).

Verse 3 emphasizes the background of greatness and divine knowledge against which the reader needs to see this act of Jesus. Jesus had all authority from the Father (see Matt. 11:27); he knew he came from God and was to be exalted to closest fellowship with the Father. Yet he washed the disciples' feet, to teach the disciples that humility and exaltation go together. He rose from the couch on which he lay at the supper table, assumed the dress of a servant (vs. 4), and began to perform the servant's task of washing the feet of the guests (vs. 5).

Verse 6 may mean that he began with Peter, who was astounded that his Teacher and Lord (vs. 13) should wash his feet: "Do *you* wash *my* feet?" He refused to permit it; even when Jesus assured him he would understand later the meaning of that humble act (vs. 7), Peter still refused to permit it. But Jesus warned Peter that unless he washed Peter's feet, Peter could have no part in his Lord's life and work (vs. 8). This was not an arbitrary ruling; unless Peter understood that the Lord was the Servant and most truly expressed his lordship precisely when he was serving his disciples, he did not share his Lord's mind and work. Appalled at the very thought of being left out of the circle of Christ's true followers, Peter went to the other extreme; he was ready for Jesus to wash not only his feet but also his hands and head (vs. 9). But Jesus said that a guest who bathes and goes to a supper needs on arrival to wash only his feet (vs. 10). A disciple, when cleansed and received into fellowship, does not need to be cleansed completely again and again; his basic commitment to Jesus has been made; he needs only to be cleansed of the dust of the road, the uncleanness that daily mars his life and witness for his Lord.

But the end of verse 10 adds another point: most of the disciples were loyal to Jesus; they all were clean except Judas. Jesus knew of his impending betrayal (vs. 11), and made a veiled reference to it by saying, "You are not all clean."

Jesus' Action an Example to His Disciples (13:12-20)

After changing from servant costume to his usual clothing, Jesus reclined again at the table (vs. 12) and explained what he had done. The disciples, he reminded them, called him Teacher and Lord, and rightly so, for he was indeed their Teacher and Lord (vs. 13). If it was in keeping with his unique and high position to wash their feet, a humble task usually done by a servant or slave, they should be equally ready to act in the same spirit (vs. 14). Jesus had given them an example, not to set them all to work washing one another's feet, but to show them the kind of action—the willing, unselfish, humble service—that they should constantly do for each other. Just as a servant ranks below his master, and a messenger (the Greek word for "messenger" is that usually translated "apostle") ranks below the one for whom he carries the message, so the disciples could not claim higher rank than Jesus or be exempt from the duty of showing humble helpfulness as he had done (compare vs. 16 with Luke 6:40 and Matt. 10:24). And the test is in action, not words; only he who *does* what Jesus teaches about humble service will have God's blessing (vs. 17).

This blessing, however, was not for all of them; Judas was still in their midst. Although Jesus chose Judas (6:70), he knew—at least now—what Judas was like and would do. Judas was eating the supper with Jesus and the other disciples, but the treachery of sharing a meal and then betraying one's comrade, referred to in Psalm 41:9, was finding its fulfillment in Judas' action on that last night of Jesus' life (vs. 18). The shock of Jesus' betrayal by one of his chosen disciples might have shattered the faith of the other disciples, but Jesus told them in advance of his betrayal, so that when it happened they would know that he was not the helpless victim of treachery but was rather the unafraid divine Son, who in all that he did was doing the Father's will and carrying out the Father's redemptive work (vs. 19). Even the betrayal, rightly understood, could deepen their faith and understanding of Jesus' nature and work. Let them catch his spirit. Let them work in the humility with which he had washed their feet. Then they will find hearers who will receive them as trustworthy witnesses to Jesus. Then a blessing will come to all who receive them, for in receiving them the people will be receiving him and the Father who sent him (vs. 20; see Matt. 10:40).

Jesus Identifies Judas as the Traitor (13:21-30)

Just as in the earlier chapters faith and unbelief, light and darkness, love and hate, have been in conflict, so in chapter 13 the shadow of betrayal has hovered over the scene (vss. 2, 10-11, 18). Now in verse 21 Jesus openly announces its imminence. It is clear from verse 22 that Judas' life as a disciple was outwardly loyal; no one knew that he was the traitor. Only Jesus knew.

Lying close to the breast of Jesus was the disciple whom Jesus loved (vs. 23). The Gospel refers to him in this way only in 13:23; 19:26-27; 20:2-10; 21:7, 20-24, and it never names him directly. But if we accept the only clear clues the Gospel gives,

we will say that he was Lazarus. (See the Introduction.) Church
tradition since the latter half of the second century, however,
has said that he was John the son of Zebedee, one of the inner
trio of the Twelve. This Gospel never mentions John by name
(see 21:2); but since later tradition named him as its author,
since 21:24 says that the beloved disciple wrote the Gospel, and
since Peter and the beloved disciple are companions in this
Gospel just as Peter and John are in Luke and Acts, the identification of the beloved disciple with John the son of Zebedee is
convincing to most Christians. But this view ignores the four-
fold emphasis of 11:3, 5, 11, 36, that Lazarus was the man for
whom Jesus had special love. It suddenly puts an entirely new
figure into the role of the disciple whom Jesus loved. Were it not
for the strong later tradition of the Church, the Gospel itself
would surely lead the reader to accept Lazarus as the beloved
disciple, and only when this is done is the Gospel a real unity:
Lazarus, Jesus' beloved disciple, is raised by Jesus and so is an
acted parable of the gospel theme of life through Christ for believers, and it is this beloved disciple who fittingly in 20:8 first
realizes clearly that Jesus has been raised from the dead.

Peter motioned to this beloved disciple to find out and tell
the others whom Jesus expected to betray him (vs. 24). The
beloved disciple leaned close to Jesus and asked in a low tone,
"Lord, who is it?" (vs. 25). Jesus did not name the traitor, but
identified him by act (vs. 26). He took a morsel of food—as a
host would do to show special favor to a guest—and gave it to
Judas the traitor; that identified him, and prepared for the fulfillment of Psalm 41:9, quoted in verse 18.

In giving the morsel to Judas did Jesus make one final appeal
for his loyalty? There is no hint of this. Jesus simply identified
him. But Judas knew from Jesus' words and act that his traitorous
intent was known, and Jesus told him to do his black deed
quickly (vs. 27). Unmasked, Judas quickly reached the final
decision to act at once. He went out to set in motion the plan to
arrest Jesus. The Gospel describes this final decision by saying
that Satan entered into Judas. So black a deed could have been
prompted only by the Devil himself.

Perhaps to explain why no one stopped Judas from going to
betray his Lord, the Gospel states in verse 28 that no one knew
why he left. (The beloved disciple knew, but he takes no initiative in this Gospel; he understands Jesus, but never takes the lead

among the disciples.) The hardly audible command of Jesus to
Judas (vs. 27) was misunderstood. Some thought that Judas, who
as treasurer for the group kept the money box, was being sent to
buy supplies for the Passover Feast to be held the next evening
(see 18:28). Others thought that Jesus had told Judas to give
some of the group's money to the poor (vs. 29). The Gospel expresses the moral blackness of Judas' deed by noting briefly that
when he went out to betray Jesus, it was night—a fitting time for
so unspeakably dark and evil a deed (vs. 30).

How Jesus Will Be Honored (13:31-35)

Once the traitor Judas had left, Jesus was with loyal disciples,
and could give them his final teaching. The time had come for
him to be glorified (vs. 31). The coming of the hour of his
Passion and exaltation had already been announced (12:23;
13:1); now, it is declared for the third time, this moment of glory
had come. His death would seem to be a defeat for him and a
humiliation for the Father, but in fact—as those with true faith
would be able to see—in his being lifted up on the cross
he would be glorified; the divine nature and power of his ministry
would be shown. The Father likewise would be glorified; his
divine presence and gracious power would be manifested to believers (vs. 32). Thus in Jesus, God would be glorified, his honor
vindicated, and his divine presence and saving power revealed;
and the Father in turn would glorify Jesus—that is, honor and
vindicate him. This vindication and honoring of the Son, this
revelation of his divine nature, would not wait until some far-off
day; it would come at once. In the very act of crucifixion, which
apparently would prove his defeat, Jesus' glory and victory and
his exaltation to the Father would be contained.

Calling the disciples "Little children" (see I John 2:1), Jesus
again indicated that the end of his ministry had come; he would
be with them but a very short time longer, and then would return to the Father, where they could not follow him yet (vs. 33;
in 14:3 Jesus indicates that later, by his help, they would be able
to follow him to his eternal home with the Father).

But his departure would not end the duty of his disciples to
do his will, and he charged them to live in mutual love (vs. 34).
He called this "a new commandment." Leviticus 19:18 shows
that love of neighbor was no new idea. What was new was that
this love was to be shown among followers of Jesus, with the

full and faithful love whose standard was the love which he had had for them throughout his ministry. This mutual Christ-like love would be the sign by which other men would recognize his disciples (vs. 35). Not verbal profession but mutual love is the real test and proof of sincere and loyal discipleship.

Peter's Denial of Jesus Predicted (13:36-38)

Jesus had spoken of going away. Peter asked where he was going (vs. 36). Jesus did not reply, as 14:28 shows he might have done, that he was going to the Father; he simply told Peter that he could not go with his Lord now but would follow him later. This need not mean, as 21:18-19 does, that Peter would later be martyred as Jesus was now to be crucified; it only means that since Jesus was leaving Peter behind in this life to witness to his Lord, Peter could not be with his Lord in glory and enjoy that heavenly fellowship with the Father until some later time. Peter was not satisfied. He did not want to be separated from his Lord; he was ready even to die for Jesus if necessary (this suggests that Peter knew that Jesus was facing or might be facing imminent death and so was offering to die with him). But Jesus knew Peter better than Peter knew himself; Peter thought he was ready to die for Jesus (vs. 37), but Jesus told him that before the night ended and the cock crowed to announce the near coming of dawn, he would deny his Lord three times (vs. 38). The sad fulfillment of this prediction comes in 18:17, 25-27.

Farewell Promises and Teaching (14:1—16:33)

Jesus the Way, the Truth, and the Life (14:1-14)

The immediate occasion for these words of comfort was the nearness of Jesus' death, which would leave the disciples shocked, shattered, and apparently alone in a hostile world. They are told that they must not give way to worry and anxiety (vs. 1). Their own resources will not be sufficient, but they must believe in God and find strength through their faith; they must also believe steadily in the crucified Jesus, through whom they have come to know the Father. They will not be left unrescued in the world; their final home will be in heaven, their Father's house, where there are many rooms (vs. 2), one for each of them. (The help the disciples will need while still in the world is promised in verse 16 and elsewhere; but first they are promised a sure final welcome with the Father.)

Some ancient manuscripts read in verse 2: "if it were not so, I would have told you. I go to prepare a place for you." But the earliest and best text, it seems, is a question: "if it were not so, would I have told you that I go to prepare a place for you?" Jesus would not have told them anything false, and it is implied that he has already told them that at his death he will go to the Father to prepare a place for them. Then, he promises, he will come and take them to be with himself (vs. 3), and because he and the Father are so closely united, they will also be with the Father.

When will Jesus come to take them? Immediately after his resurrection? At the death of each of them? At the last day? Probably Jesus means here his coming at the last day, but this does not exclude his presence with and help to his disciples at earlier times.

In verse 4 Jesus says that they know the way to the place where he is going, and verse 2 has indicated that the place is his Father's house. But Thomas says that they do not know the destination and so cannot know the way (vs. 5). Jesus replies that he is "the way" (vs. 6). The way is not just a road: it is this central Person; through him they come to the Father. He adds that he is "the truth," for he is "full of grace and truth" (1:14, 17), all who determine to do his will will know the truth (8:31-32), and he is the living embodiment of truth. He is also "the life" (1:4), and gives new and true life to those who by faith feed on his life-giving bread (6:35; 11:25). But the emphasis here is on Jesus as the way to the Father, and that is why one version has translated the sentence, "I am the true and living way." As the Light and Savior of all men, Jesus is the only way to the Father; men come to the Father through him. Those who really know him know the Father; and the disciples, after knowing him through his ministry, surely know and have seen the Father by knowing and seeing Jesus.

No doubt the disciples should know the Father, but Philip still feels that the Father has not been clearly revealed to them (vs. 8). He realizes that to know the Father is the all-important thing, so he asks Jesus to show them the Father; that will satisfy all their need and questions. With surprise Jesus asks whether he has been so long with them and they still do not know him. To see Jesus—that is, to perceive who he really is and what his words and works really mean—is to see the Father present and active (vs. 9). The Father and the Son are so closely linked that to see and be in touch with one is to see and be in touch with the other. Jesus never teaches or acts independently, as though he alone were the final authority; the Father dwelling in Jesus does his works—both teaching and signs—through Jesus (vs. 10). Between the Father and Jesus the Son there is complete union and harmony of life and purpose. If the disciples understand that, they will know that to know either the Father or the Son is to know both. But if they are still weak in faith and understanding (and in this Gospel faith and understanding go together), they should look at the remarkable works which Jesus does (vs. 11). These works, signs of God's power present and operative in Jesus, should lead them at least to a second-class faith that may hold them to Jesus until they come to the full faith that needs no signs to support its glad and steady loyalty to the Father and the Son (see 20:29).

But it is not only Jesus who can do remarkable deeds. Every believer will receive power to do not only what Jesus has done, but even still greater works (vs. 12). These works will no doubt include not only such remarkable miracles as the Gospel reports were done by Jesus, but also the gathering of great numbers of believers into the one flock to which Jesus looked forward (10:16). The disciples will not be able to do these greater works by their own strength, or even during Jesus' lifetime. Only when Jesus has been exalted to the Father, when the Spirit has made available to his followers the benefits of his death, resurrection, and exaltation, will this become possible. Even then it will be possible only through the ministry of the Son. They must ask him (note that they may pray to the Son; compare Acts 7:59), and when they ask him in faith he will do whatever they ask (vss. 13-14). Thus the Father will receive praise and honor through this ministry which the Son exercises for and through his followers. The Son thus glorifies the Father not only by his ministry during his earthly life but also by working through his followers after his exaltation.

The promise is amazingly comprehensive: "whatever you ask," "if you ask anything." This does not mean that selfish, unworthy requests will be granted. It means that Christ will

answer all prayers offered in his "name," that is, with an appeal
to Jesus and his work and with loyal dedication to God's will
as Jesus has made it known. Verse 14 repeats the promise of
verse 13 in order to emphasize the certainty that such prayers will
surely be answered. The promise is not merely to church officers,
or to ordained ministers, but to the disciples as a group.

The First Promise to Give the Spirit (14:15-17)

Prayer "in my name" implies dedication and obedience to
Christ; verse 15 makes this point explicit. Those who love him
will express their love and faith by keeping his commandments
after he has gone to the Father. They will do this even more
faithfully than they do now. That fuller obedience will be possible
because they will not be left alone. The Counselor, the Holy
Spirit, will be given to them (vs. 16); Jesus the Son will return to
them in a new form (vs. 18); the Father will be with them (vs.
23). The full presence, leading, power, and blessing of God will
give them adequate resources for loyal obedience and a faithful
ministry to others.

The gift of the Holy Spirit is promised in 14:16-17, 26; 15:26;
16:7-13 (see 1:33; 7:39). While the Spirit of God is mentioned
in the Old Testament and in the Synoptic Gospels as present and
active before Jesus' death and resurrection, in this Gospel the
Spirit is the gift of the exalted Jesus; he interprets and continues
the work of Jesus. All earlier work of the Spirit pales into in-
significance before the powerful and effective work of the Spirit
in interpreting and continuing Jesus' work. The Christian will
always know the Spirit as the gift of the risen Christ or, to put
it in other words, as the gift of the Father at the request of the
risen Christ. Jesus will be taken from the disciples after a rather
brief ministry, but the Spirit will remain with them and dwell in
them so that they never have to face life alone.

Verses 16-17 contain two titles of the Spirit. The Greek word
for "Counselor" means literally a legal helper, an advocate. In
I John 2:1 it is used of the risen Christ, our Advocate with the
Father. Here it describes the work of the Spirit as that of an ad-
viser and helper, an encourager, comforter, and inspirer, a constant companion of the believer. The second title is "the Spirit of
truth" (see 15:26; 16:13). The Spirit is not merely true and
honest but teaches the truth and guides believers to know, witness
to, and express in life the truth about God and his Son Jesus

Christ. The hostile or indifferent world cannot know or receive the Spirit, but believers, because they love Christ and keep his commandments, will receive the Spirit at the request of Christ the Son to the Father.

The Believer's Union with Both Father and Son (14:18-24)

Verses 16-17 might seem to mean that after his death Jesus will be absent from his disciples. Verses 18-21 correct that impression. He will not leave them orphans, that is, friendless and desolate; he will come to them, perhaps in part in the coming of the Spirit to continue his work, but also in his own return to them, at the Resurrection as well as at the last day. Verse 19 suggests that he here thinks particularly of a return to them just after the Resurrection. After a short time they will see him; they then will know that he lives and has life-giving power, for he will give to his loyal believers the gift of true life. They then will realize clearly not only that Jesus lives in unbreakable union with his Father but also that they live in a close fellowship of mutual love with him (vs. 20).

But this fellowship is not just a mystical thrill. They will enjoy it because they remember and obey the commandments he has given them; they will express their love for him by their obedience (vs. 21). Such loyal love will receive a double blessing: the Father himself will love them, and Jesus will love them and appear to them to reassure them that he as well as the Spirit is constantly with them. He will be present not merely through the Spirit, but also in direct presence, though not in the visible form of his earthly ministry.

In verses 22-24 Jesus clarifies his point for Judas, called "son of James" in Luke 6:16; Acts 1:13. Judas—not the traitor Iscariot, who left the group at 13:30—asks how Jesus will manifest himself to his disciples but not to the world (vs. 22). Jesus explains that he will not return in a visible, physical form that any unbeliever could see. Only those who love him and show that love by obedience to his teaching will discern his personal presence. The Father will love them, and both the Father and the exalted Jesus will come and dwell with them (vs. 23). This refers not simply to a Resurrection appearance or to the final coming at the last day, but to steady companionship with believers during their life of faith and service to Christ.

Verse 24 emphasizes two thoughts: Lack of love for Jesus is

shown in failure to keep his commandments, and he teaches exactly what the Father has sent him to teach.

The Second Promise to Give the Spirit (14:25-26)

While both the risen Jesus and the Father will be with the loyal disciples in the coming days, the divine presence and action are to be expressed chiefly through the Spirit. Jesus has taught them during his earthly life (vs. 25), but the Counselor (see vs. 16), whom the Father will send in Jesus' name—that is, at Jesus' request and to act in his place—will continue and complete Jesus' teaching ministry (vs. 26). He will recall what Jesus has taught and help the disciples to understand it; he will teach still further needed truth—"all things" that they need to know to live and to serve their Lord rightly. All that he teaches will include and be true to what Jesus has taught and done during his earthly life.

The Peace the Exalted Son Will Give (14:27-31)

Verse 27 returns to the thought of verse 1. The disciples need not be troubled because Jesus must meet death and so can no longer walk with them in his former manner. He leaves with them his peace, his steady trust in the Father, his superiority to outward troubles. Such poise and quiet confidence the disobedient world does not know and cannot give. But the disciples will know it from their past life with him and from his continued gifts to them, particularly from the gift of the Spirit and from Jesus' renewed presence with them.

Verses 28-31 are a gentle reminder that in their anxiety the disciples have been thinking too much about themselves. They should rejoice at the word that he is going to his Father (vs. 28); this will mean glory and privilege for Jesus and also greater blessings for the disciples as the exalted Christ and the Father act together to help them and support their Christian witness. Verse 29 points out a benefit which his teaching about his death will bring them later. By telling them about his death beforehand, he shows that it will not surprise or defeat him. His foreknowledge of events will become clear to them when the events happen; they will see that all things fit into God's redemptive plan. Jesus' quiet acceptance of what is coming will lead to the deepening of their faith. They already believe, and this will help them to believe with a deeper, steadier, more intelligent faith.

The crisis is close at hand (vs. 30). Satan is called "the ruler of this world," but his apparent control of it is a hollow rule which Jesus' death and exaltation will overthrow. He is coming in the person of Judas, into whom he has entered (13:27) to set actively in motion the arrest of Jesus. He has no real power over Jesus (nor has Pilate, 19:11); Jesus is faithfully following the Father's saving plan in order to open the way to eternal life for believers and also to show the world, if it will only open its eyes, that Jesus loves the Father and is completely dedicated to doing what the Father has sent him to do (vs. 31). After these words of assurance, instruction, love, and filial obedience to the Father, Jesus asks the disciples to rise and leave the room where they have eaten the Last Supper.

Jesus the True Vine (15:1-11)

The teaching in 15:1-11 that Jesus is the True Vine, and that his disciples are the branches, has given great comfort to Christians. But in some ways it is a sobering passage. The Old Testament more than once describes Israel as God's vineyard (Isa. 5:1-7) or vine (Ps. 80:8; Ezek. 19:10-14), but it also announces judgment on Israel for its sin of unfruitfulness. In the same way, in this Gospel the unfruitful branch is pruned off; unless the disciple abides faithfully in Jesus he will be cast forth as a worthless branch and burned (vss. 2, 6). Even the fruitful branch must be pruned or disciplined (vs. 2). Abiding in the love of Jesus is defined as keeping his commandments (vs. 10); only to the obedient life are blessings promised. These verses promise no automatic blessing; they set up a stern standard which requires faithful obedience to Christ.

Yet the privilege promised is a rich one. To be a branch of the vine is to live in fellowship with Jesus the True Vine and under the watchful care of the Father, the Vinedresser of his vineyard or people (vs. 1). The Father intelligently uses discipline to make possible greater fruitfulness in his service (vs. 2). The teaching of Jesus has cleansed or pruned the disciples so that they may be steadily fruitful (vs. 3). By their own will and action they must abide in him (vs. 4; the illustration is not adequate here; a branch cannot rebel and go off and leave the main vine, but a person can rebel and break his tie with Jesus and so lose the source of life and strength). If the disciples do abide in him by steady, grateful faith and by faithful doing of his will, they will have a richly fruitful life in the service of God; but they must remember that it is only by their link with Jesus, by the life and power he gives them, that they achieve these results. The fruit is never due to their own independent power (vs. 5).

Among the promised blessings of a life linked with Jesus is answer to prayer (vs. 7). Whatever they ask will be granted. But there are two conditions. One is that they abide in him by unwavering faith in him and complete commitment to him; the other is that his words, his teachings, abide in them, so that their thought, purpose, and prayers are shaped by complete dedication to him and by full loyalty to what he has taught them.

Certainly one petition which disciples will include in such loyal prayer will be that they may yield much fruit in their life of obedience and service; they will want to serve God, to bring honor to him, and to lead men to see that he is truly God and has sent his Son to be the Savior of the world (4:42). Their fruitful lives will bring glory to God and their obedience will prove that they are loyal disciples of Jesus; obedience is the test of discipleship (vs. 8). Jesus has loved them as the Father has loved him, and they are to abide in his love for them (vs. 9). How will they abide in his love for them? How will this abiding show itself? By keeping his commandments, by staying gratefully within the circle of his love for them, just as Jesus has kept his Father's commandments and lived in the full fellowship of love with his Father (vs. 10). They are to take Jesus' perfect loyalty and love as the standard for their own lives (see Matt. 5:48).

We have said that in one way this is a sobering passage. It requires the disciples to accept discipline, to dedicate life to the fruitful doing of God's will, to stay close to Jesus, to keep his words in mind and heart and live by them, to keep his commandments. His teaching is demanding. But it opens the way to joy, for they will find true satisfaction only by living touch with Jesus and by willing obedience to his teaching. Their joy will be like the joy of Christ who did his Father's will; it will be a joy full and never to be regretted (vs. 11).

Life in Love and Obedience (15:12-17)

If all the disciples abide in Jesus, they all are part of the one vine, the one People of God. Thus, they are bound not only to Jesus but also to one another through their tie with Jesus. To be in Christ means to live in the fellowship of his disciples in his Church. So they must love one another, with a full love and loyalty like that which Jesus has shown toward them (vs. 12). How much has he loved them? With the greatest love: enough to die for them (vs. 13). He is facing death within a few hours, not for show but to do his Father's will and to benefit his followers. He is laying down his life for his friends, and these disciples are his friends *if*—an important if—they do what he commands them by loving one another and by living in steady loyalty to him (vs. 14).

In the past, Jesus implies, he has called them his "servants." (The Greek word can mean "slaves," and this translation would express well his complete authority over his disciples; but it might suggest unwilling and abject servitude, whereas true disciples follow Jesus willingly. And so it seems better to translate the Greek word by the English word "servants.") The servant merely takes orders and is not fully informed as to what his master is doing. But Jesus has told his disciples all that the Father has sent him to teach; all along he has really treated them not as mere servants, bound to take orders and fulfill them without understanding them, but as friends who understand what is wanted and act with intelligent readiness to do the will of their Friend. So from now on, he says, he will openly call them his friends (vs. 15).

The disciples are indeed the friends of Jesus their Lord. But they are not his equals. They did not choose him to be their leader; he chose them, and appointed them to carry out his purpose (vs. 16). If they carry out that purpose they have the promise that the good results of that work will abide; what they achieve will bring a permanent blessing not only to themselves but also to those whom they serve. They have also another promise: as they live fruitful lives they may pray to the Father to meet their needs, and the Father will answer their prayers. Here again, as in verse 7, it is implied that they will pray in loyalty to Christ and with the intent to use God's gifts to carry out their work for Christ; then they will ask for the right things and they will receive every blessing they need to sustain and prosper them in their work.

Verse 17 returns to the teaching of verse 12; as Jesus' friends who keep his commandments, who are not mere servants but trusted friends, whom he has chosen and to whom he has promised every needed help in their work, the disciples must continually love one another. (The present tense of the Greek imperative verb commands each disciple to give steady, unfailing love to each of his fellow disciples.)

The World's Hate for Christ and His Disciples (15:18-25)

Verses 18-25 introduce a darker note. Verses 12-17 have described the life of the disciples as an immense privilege. Even though it makes great demands, it is a privilege to be friends of Christ and constantly serve him. But such a life will bring upon them the hostility of the unbelieving world. They must remember that Jesus has met hostility and now faces death as the outcome of his good works and vital teaching. Those who serve him may expect the same hate and ill-treatment (vs. 18). They have broken with the world, that is, the network of persons and forces hostile to Christ; and so the world hates them as it does Christ. He has chosen them; they have responded in faith, and have come out of the world into the fellowship of believers. Because they have disowned the world and actively oppose it, it hates them (vs. 19).

Are the disciples expecting that though Jesus will suffer, they will be excused? He clears away that misunderstanding. Using a proverb, that a servant is not greater than his master (and so cannot expect better treatment than his master receives), he warns them that they will share his lot—both persecution from those who reject his message and loyal response from those who accept it (vs. 20). Why will the people in the evil world reject the message of Jesus and the disciples? Because they do not know the Father who sent Jesus and who rightly claims the obedience of the disciples (vs. 21). But such people cannot plead ignorance as an excuse for their unbelief and hostility to Christ. What follows overlooks their failure to heed Moses and the prophets (see Luke 16:29-31) and concentrates upon the world's greater sin of rejecting their greater opportunity to believe in Jesus. They would have no sin and guilt if Jesus had not come with the gospel truth and offered them salvation; opportunity not accepted brings guilt (vs. 22). But his coming, preaching, and works of divine power take away their excuse and leave them obviously guilty of sin in rejecting the message of God which Jesus brought. Nor can they say that they love God but hate Jesus. The Father sent Jesus, and to reject and hate Jesus is to reject and hate the Father also (vss. 23-24). The way they act fulfills what is said in the Old Testament (Pss. 35:19; 69:4); to hate Jesus without proper cause is to act just as the psalmist's enemies did (vs. 25). For the Gospel writer to find such an unhappy event predicted in Scripture meant to him that such hate did not surprise or defeat God; in some way it served a constructive role in the divine plan and work.

The Third Promise to Give the Spirit (15:26-27)

According to 14:16, 26, the Counselor, the Holy Spirit, is to be with the disciples permanently, remind them of all that Jesus has taught, and teach them all things. In 15:26 the Counselor is again called the Spirit of truth (compare 14:17); he not only is faithfully true to the Father but is active in promoting and defending the divine truth and purpose. His special mission is to bear witness to Jesus and to Jesus' divine mission and work. In 14:16, 26 Jesus says that he will pray the Father to send the Spirit. In 15:26 he says that he will send the Spirit from the Father. There is no contradiction. The Father and the Son both have a part in sending the Spirit to be with the disciples. Jesus does not mean that he alone will send the Spirit; as if to guard against such a misunderstanding, he says that he will send the Spirit "from the Father," and adds that the Spirit "proceeds from the Father." The Spirit is as closely linked with the Father as with the Son; that the Spirit is no mere angelic messenger but is fully divine is implied in all that this Gospel says of him.

It must be remembered that verses 18-25 have spoken frankly about the world's hate for Jesus and for the disciples. So the witness of the Spirit in verse 26 is a witness in the face of the world's hostility. The Spirit will oppose the world's hate and misrepresentation of Jesus (so also in 16:7-11); he will oppose the world by bearing witness to Jesus. The disciples must give the same witness (vs. 27). Even though they face hostility and hate, they must steadfastly witness to Jesus as the Christ, the Son of God (20:31), the Savior of the world (4:42), who came to give eternal life to all who believe (3:16, 36). The disciples present at the Last Supper are the very ones who can do this. They have been with Jesus from the beginning of his ministry; they know his message, have seen his works, and have recognized in them signs of his divine person and power and mission. Their privilege places on them the responsibility to preach continually and fearlessly the gospel message which centers in Jesus.

The Coming Persecution of the Disciples (16:1-4a)

The theme of the world's hostility to Jesus and the disciples
continues into chapter 16. In verses 1-4 Jesus tells the disciples
why he has told them that they must suffer. He has warned them
in advance so that when the world persecutes them they will not
be surprised and discouraged and so give up their faith (vs. 1).
Hard days lie ahead (vs. 2); other Jews, who refuse to believe in
Jesus as their Christ, will expel the disciples from the synagogues
and Jewish community life. At times the hostility to the disciples
will become so fierce that some will suffer martyrdom, and the
persecutors will mistakenly think that by killing the disciples they
are rendering a religious service to God and to their people. If they
really knew the Father, and recognized Jesus as the Christ, the
Son of God, they would not persecute his disciples; but this is
their tragic fault—they do not really know the Father nor recognize who Jesus really is (vs. 3). When such hardship comes, the
disciples are to remember that Jesus foresaw and foretold it;
this will help to steady them while they suffer (vs. 4a).

The Fourth Promise to Give the Spirit (16:4b-15)

While Jesus was with his disciples during his ministry, he did
not need to forewarn them of such future hardships; by his
presence and guidance he could give them help as they needed it
(vs. 4b). But now he tells them of all this impending trouble because he is about to leave them and return to the Father who
sent him. He then says that none of them is asking him where
he is going. (This is perhaps the strongest argument for changing
the position of chapters 15 and 16; if these chapters were moved,
for example, to a position in 13:31, just after the words "Jesus
said," this statement in 16:5 that the disciples have not asked him
where he is going would fit better, whereas in the present order
of the chapters the disciples have already asked him about this
twice, in 13:36 and 14:5.) The disciples feel crushed and down-
cast at the word of Jesus' departure, as though no good could
come from it (vs. 6). But apart from the position of honor and
authority to which he is going (a point not mentioned here), it
will be to their advantage for him to depart, for only if he de-
parts can he send to them the Counselor, the Holy Spirit (vs. 7).

The work of the Spirit as here described has two aspects (vss.
8-11 and 12-15). For one thing, as in 15:26, he will witness to

Jesus in the face of the world's hostility to Jesus and the disciples. At least partly through the Spirit-inspired preaching of Christian leaders, the Holy Spirit will convince or convict the unbelieving world that its attitude toward Jesus has been wrong. He will do this in three respects: First, he will convict the world that it sinned in not believing in Jesus (vs. 9). Just when the world will realize or admit its sin Jesus does not say, but he clearly states that the Spirit will take the offensive and sooner or later will force the world to recognize that it was wicked not to believe that Jesus was sent by the Father and so was entitled to faith and obedience. Second, he will convict the world of righteousness (vs. 10), because Jesus, when crucified, will be raised from the dead and exalted to the Father, and so, while he will no longer be visible to his followers, he will be vindicated and shown to be what he claimed to be and what the disciples witness that he is: the Christ, the Son of God, sent by the Father and entitled to faith and obedience. Third, the Spirit will convict the world of judgment (vs. 11). The death of Jesus will no longer seem to be the defeat and discrediting of Jesus; in it the Spirit will compel men to see God's judgment on sin and particularly on Satan, the apparent ruler of this present hostile world (compare 12:31).

Verses 12-15 mention a second aspect of the Spirit's work. He will guide the disciples into all the truth (see 14:26). During his rather short ministry Jesus could not teach the disciples all that they would need to know; he could teach them only what they could understand and accept at their stage of spiritual growth. The Spirit of truth, always trustworthy and dependable, will carry forward Jesus' work, speaking only what he hears from the Father and so giving the disciples all the truth they need to know for their own good and for their daily ministry. Whatever they need to know about the unknown future he will also make known to them (vs. 13). He will never disown or repudiate what Jesus has taught; he will always glorify Jesus by witnessing to him and carrying forward his ministry; what he teaches will be what he has received from the Son (vs. 14).

In verse 13 "whatever he hears" refers to what the Spirit hears from the Father; in verse 14 the Spirit "will take what is mine [that is, Christ's teaching and work] and declare it to you." Verse 15 unites these two ideas: the Son shares the Father's purpose and truth, and so when the Spirit teaches what the Father wants him to teach, he is at the same time teaching and explaining what

Jesus has taught; he is continuing in a fuller and more widely outreaching form the work and teaching of Jesus the Son.

Through Sorrow to Eternal Joy (16:16-24)

Verse 16 states the theme which the next verses will explain. Jesus' death is very near; in a little while the disciples will see him no more in his present body. But after a very short time they will see him again. This might be thought to suggest that after a very short period of history the end would come and Jesus would come to the disciples and take them to be with him and the Father forever. But the main and perhaps the only idea in this section is that after his death, which is just at hand, the disciples will pass through a short time of dark sorrow, and then the Resurrection will bring him back to them, so that their sorrow will be turned into eternal joy.

As often happens in this Gospel, the ambiguous statement of verse 16 is at first misunderstood. The disciples are puzzled (vss. 17-18); as in the Synoptic Gospels, where they never understand the necessity or benefit of Jesus' death until after his death and resurrection, so here they ask one another what he means by this cryptic statement. He knows what they are asking one another (vs. 19); he always knows what they are thinking and saying. So he explains further (vs. 20). They will go through a (short) period of weeping, when the world will seem to have triumphed over Jesus and his cause by putting him to death. But this short period of sorrow will be turned into wonderful joy when the weeping over his death is taken away by his resurrection and manifest victory over the sinful and now defeated world. This reversal Jesus then explains by a parable (vs. 21). A woman has pain and sorrow when giving birth to her child, but after the short period of birth pains her anguish is past, her sorrow forgotten, and she rejoices in possessing the child that has been born. In the same way the lonely disciples will grieve over the death of Jesus, but in a short time he will see them again at the Resurrection, and then they will rejoice with a joy that the opposition of the world and the hardships of life cannot take from them (vs. 22). They will live henceforth in a spirit of joy and victory and will have the needed power to serve him.

In that day, when they see the risen Christ and receive the gift of lasting joy, they will also have a fuller understanding of what life through faith in Christ means (compare 2:22; 12:16).

Guided by the Spirit of truth (vs. 13), they will not need to ask Jesus further questions but will have the knowledge they need to live good and loyal lives. They may ask God for anything they need and he will certainly give it to them—if they ask in the name of Jesus, that is, as his disciples who gratefully remember all he has done for them and ask God's gifts to use in Christian witness and living (vs. 23). While he has been with them, they have not prayed to the Father in the name of Jesus. That has not been proper or necessary; Jesus himself has cared for them and watched over them. But in that new day they will be able to pray with confidence as long as they pray in a believing, loyal, and unselfish spirit; and the rich answer to their prayer will make their joy overflow (vs. 24).

The Father's Love for the Disciples (16:25-28)

When Jesus says that he has been speaking to the disciples in figures (vs. 25)—that is, in figurative language that is hard to understand clearly—he does not mean that he has deliberately tried to keep them from understanding him. He means that to help them at their stage of spiritual growth he has had to use such illustrations. Even then they have not fully understood him. But the hour is soon coming, after he has risen and given them the Holy Spirit, when he will be able to give them plain teaching concerning the Father and they will understand it far better than they can now. And he reassures them (vss. 26-27) that when in his name they ask things in prayer, the Father will answer them; the Son will not need to pray to the Father for them. The Son will not be indifferent to their prayers, but since the Father loves them and is eager to help them, the Son will not need to urge the Father to answer the disciples' prayers. The Father loves them; he knows that they have loved Jesus and have believed that the Father sent Jesus; and so the Father will be ready to answer their prayers, bless their lives, and support them in their Christian life of obedience and witness to the Son.

Jesus adds in verse 28 that he came from the Father—he is the pre-existent Son, divine in nature and sent by God; he has come into the world—"the Word became flesh" (1:14); he is about to leave this earthly way of life he has been living in the world—his cross looms just ahead; and he is going to the Father—coupled with his cross is to be his exaltation to glory and active lordship.

The Victory of Jesus Over the World (16:29-33)

The disciples consider Jesus' statement plain and clear (vs. 29). They are ready to say that Jesus knows all things, can teach effectively without questions or help from others, and came from the Father—that is, that he is the divine Son of God become flesh (vs. 30). But is their faith full and adequate? They no doubt think so, and verse 31 may be not a question but a statement: As far as your present intention is concerned, you believe. But Jesus knows that when he is arrested, their faith and courage will be tested. That hour is so near that he can say it "has come" (vs. 32); when it comes, they will leave him and flee in fear and panic. As far as human companionship and help are concerned, they will leave him alone. But because he and the Father are one (10:30), he is never alone. He will meet that crisis in union with the Father; what he does for men's salvation will be the Father's work as well as his.

Jesus has told the disciples of their coming failure (vs. 32). He did not do so to unnerve them or to take away their steadiness or inner peace. Quite the contrary, as verse 33 says. When they desert him, as he knows they will, the fact that he had foreseen their failure will convince them that he is superior to their failures and fickleness and that he loves them in spite of their need for his forgiveness. So even in their experience of failure they need not despair, but they must see that their source of renewal and strength is only in him and in the help he brings from the Father; if they see that and gratefully accept it, they then may have peace and be of good cheer, knowing that though the world may intimidate and defeat them, it cannot intimidate or defeat Jesus. He has overcome the world by his loyal faithfulness to the Father and his willingness to suffer for their sake; they can have victory if they keep their faith in him.

Jesus Prays for Himself and His Disciples (17:1-26)

The Last Supper closes with a prayer in which Jesus prays first for himself (vss. 1-5), then for the disciples who are with him (vss. 6-19), and finally for those who will believe through the witness to him which these disciples give (vss. 20-26).

Jesus Prays for Himself (17:1-5)

Jesus lifts his eyes to heaven (vs. 1); through this familiar attitude (11:41) he expresses the fact that in prayer the worshiper reverently recognizes how great and transcendent God is. As the unique Son, Jesus addresses God as his Father; his close tie with the Father is vastly more intimate than that which believers express in the words of the Lord's Prayer (Matt. 6:9). "Father" here expresses also Jesus' trust and his confidence that his prayer will be answered. Once more he says that the hour of his death has come. He accepts that death as the Father's will, but he prays that in that death and resulting resurrection the Father will glorify the Son, giving him victory over Satan and the world and exalting him to close fellowship with the Father. In that redeeming death and triumphant resurrection the Son will bring honor and praise to the Father by fulfilling the Father's will. When he became flesh (1:14) he received power over all flesh, that is, over all mankind, and it was the Father's will that the Son should give eternal life to all whom the Father had chosen and given to him to save and keep and bring together in the Church (vs. 2).

What is eternal life? This Gospel has spoken of it repeatedly, but has never defined it. Now Jesus gives the one definition of it which the Gospel contains (vs. 3). Eternal life is to know the Father as the only true God and Jesus Christ as his Son who has been sent by the Father to carry out the divine purpose. To "know" God in this Gospel does not mean merely to know about him; it means to know him by living in a reverent, believing, loyal relation to him, so that in actual life one knows him as Father and knows the Son as Savior and Lord. To know the Father and the Son is to be bound to them in a close and blessed fellowship in which the believer continuously receives the gift of life and the power to live as God wants him to live. This is eternal life: to know God through Jesus Christ and to live in grateful faith and loyal obedience. The true believer will find it his joy to do this, both in this earthly life and in the coming age. Thus rightly related to Father and Son, the believer has this eternal privilege: he has nothing to fear from either death or the Last Judgment. He has already entered into life.

During his ministry Jesus has carried out faithfully the Father's will (vs. 4). By doing fully what the Father sent him to do, he has led all men of faith to honor and praise the Father. He has always

done "what is pleasing to him" (8:29). Now that the hour of death
is at hand, the Son prays that he may enjoy the same glory he
formerly had with the Father in the long reaches of time, far
back before the world was created (vs. 5). This clearly states the
pre-existence of the Son—a point repeatedly attested in this
Gospel (1:1; 8:58; 16:28). The divine Son had shared in the
glorious divine life before he entered into human life (1:14); he
prays that having completed the work he had come to do he may
be given again that unique and honored position with the Father
that he had enjoyed from all eternity.

Jesus Prays for His Disciples (17:6-19)

Jesus next turns his prayer to the needs of his disciples (vss.
6-19). He recalls that he has "manifested" the Father's name to
them; that is, he has made known to them the Father's presence,
nature, and will. He adds that they have been his disciples, not
because they were clever enough to choose that privilege, nor
merely because Jesus chose them, but ultimately because the
Father had given them to Jesus as his followers; the secret of
their choice and salvation is God's original choice and his active
call given to them through Jesus. They were the Father's people; the
Father gave them to Jesus as his followers and friends; and they
have received Jesus' teaching, believed in him, and kept his
word (vs. 6). They have recognized that Jesus' teaching and
mission had their origin in God; they have believed and confessed that he was sent by the Father to teach what he taught
and to do what he did (vss. 7-8).

These disciples are the Father's own family and so are also
Jesus' own brothers or friends (vs. 10). Jesus must now leave
them in the world to carry on the Father's work by witnessing to
Jesus as the Christ, the Son of God (vs. 11). He earnestly prays
for them (vs. 9). He does not pray for the hostile and unrespon-
sive world. This Gospel concentrates on the relation between
Jesus and his disciples. He prays for these disciples. They have
special need of his prayer and of divine help, for he can no
longer live with them in daily visible companionship and teach
them what it means to believe and live in love and obedience. They
will be left in the hostile world, which can no longer attack Jesus
directly but will attack him by opposing and attacking his disciples. He will be exalted to his place with the Father, and they
will be left to witness to him in the face of the world's stubborn

unbelief (vs. 11). Therefore they need the Father's special pro-
tection and care, and for that care Jesus prays. The Father who
chose them and gave them to Jesus as his disciples will surely
hear this prayer and keep them from evil life, from failure of
courage, and from defeat. Part of the blessing of that care is
noted: that they may be as vitally one as the Father and the Son
are one (see 10:30). They cannot stand firm against the world
unless by the Father's care they stand united in common faith
and mutual love.

During Jesus' ministry he kept the disciples in the Father's
name. Acting for the Father and recognizing in them the Father's
own people, Jesus has made God's nature and will known to
them (vs. 12). He has guarded them from danger, and none of
them has been lost to the hostile world except Judas, "the son of
perdition," the one follower who in God's mysterious plan was
destined to be lost and was marked out in Scripture as destined for
this shameful lot (Ps. 41:9). To the Gospel writer this prophetic
forecast that Judas would betray Jesus means that this betrayal
did not defeat God's purpose or surprise God but in some way
had a constructive place in God's plan.

Now that Jesus is returning to the Father and will no longer
live in daily visible companionship with his disciples, they will
need the Father's special care, and Jesus speaks of this in his
prayer so that they will be clearly aware of his concern for them
and will await with confidence the active love and certain pro-
tection which the Father will give them (vs. 13). Knowing all
this, they need not be shaken or defeated by his departure;
understanding the meaning of the apparently devastating events
that are just ahead, they will be able not only to withstand
the shock but also to recognize the saving work which God
has done through the Cross. So they will see victory and find
joy in apparent defeat; they will have in perfect fullness the
same joy that Jesus knows in doing the will of the Father, even
when it means accepting the Cross.

Jesus has given the disciples far more than this final assurance
of the Father's care; he has already given them the Father's
"word," the entire message which the Father sent him to teach
them (vs. 14). This assurance and preparation they will greatly
need. Already the hostile world has directed its hate at them.
The world has seen that by believing in Jesus the disciples have
renounced the hostile, God-opposed world and have given their

loyalty to God and his Son; so the world has hated them. Jesus cannot pray for the Father to take the disciples out of the world, for it is their task to carry forward his work by their faithful witness to him. So they must stay in the world and witness to the world, and Jesus prays that as they do this they may not be taken captive by the evil spirit of the world and by its evil leader, Satan (vs. 15).

The disciples, like Jesus, do not belong to the evil world (vs. 16); they are dedicated to worship and serve the Father by their Christian life and witness. They need still deeper and fuller sanctification (vs. 17); they need to understand, accept, and live fully the message which the Father through Jesus has given them; they need to be completely consecrated in order to live out in their own lives and present in their teaching the divine truth given by Jesus and embodied in his life (1:14; 14:6). The disciples are never called "apostles" in this Gospel, but the word, which means persons sent on a mission, expresses what the disciples are to be; as the Father has sent Jesus (see Heb. 3:1), Jesus now sends them into the world to carry out their ministry for him (vs. 18). For them, and also for the others mentioned in verse 20, he now consecrates himself in death on the cross; his purpose is that they, in turn, may be truly and fully consecrated to a sacrificial ministry in his name and spirit (vs. 19).

Jesus Prays for All Believers (17:20-26)

In the third part of the prayer (vss. 20-26), Jesus looks forward to the people who will believe in him through the witness of the disciples. As this witness spreads and the Church grows, it may be increasingly difficult for his followers to be one in spirit and mutual love. So he prays for the unity of the entire Church (vs. 21), and not for a merely lukewarm or formal unity, but for a vital unity as real and close as that which exists between the Father and the Son, a mutual indwelling in which each lives in the other and both are one. Then—and only then—the world will believe that the Father has sent Jesus and that the gospel is true. In such a unity with Father and Son and with one another, something of the divine glory that the Son has already given them will shine out in rich splendor (vs. 22). In that glory they will "become" the unity for which Jesus prays (vs. 23). This is not a human possibility; it will only come by the divine presence working in the Church. When they find such perfect unity, with Christ in them and the Father in Christ, the world will know that the Father has sent his Son to be the Savior of the world (4:42) and that he has loved the disciples just as truly as he has loved Jesus his Son (vs. 23).

Looking beyond the gift of divine glory to the disciples during their earthly life in the one Church, Jesus goes on to pray that these disciples, given to him by the Father, may finally have the privilege of being with him in heavenly glory and beholding the full glory of the Son (vs. 24). That glory, enjoyed before the creation of the world (vs. 5), and given up as Jesus entered human life (1:14), will be restored by the exaltation won through the Cross and its victory.

In one final, summary look at his ministry (vss. 25-26), Jesus, addressing the Father as righteous (compare "holy Father," vs. 11), confesses with regret that the hostile world has not known the Father; but he emphasizes that he has known the Father and that through his life and teaching his disciples have come to know that the Father has sent him. He has made known the Father's name—that is, he has made known not merely the formal name or mere existence of the Father, but the Father's nature and purpose and demand—and he promises, as he faces his cross, that now in his death he will make the Father known in a unique way (vs. 26). His aim in this act of obedient suffering is so to make known the Father's nature and will that the divine love the Father has shown him may find its home in the disciples and that Jesus may find his home in their hearts. Jesus has made the love of God real to them, and as Jesus dwells in their lives they will know that God's love has taken possession of them, to uphold them in their Christian witness and to bless them in their Christian lives.

THE GLORY AND VICTORY OF JESUS REVEALED IN HIS DEATH AND RESURRECTION

John 18:1—20:29

The Betrayal and Arrest of Jesus (18:1-11)

Chapters 18-20 contain the Passion and Resurrection story; they tell of the betrayal, arrest, trial, crucifixion, burial, and resurrection of Jesus. After the Last Supper (ch. 13), farewell

talks (chs. 14-16), and closing prayer (ch. 17), Jesus led the
disciples out of Jerusalem by the east gate, went down the slope,
and crossed the Brook Kidron to the lower slopes of the Mount of
Olives (vs. 1). There he entered "a garden"—perhaps a grove of
olive trees, since Matthew 26:36 and Mark 14:32 call the place
"Gethsemane" ("oil-press"), which suggests that olives were
grown there and that a press had been built to press out the
olive oil.

Judas knew the place and was aware that Jesus often met there
with his disciples (vs. 2). This recalls the fact that in this Gospel
Jesus has visited Jerusalem often and spent much time there
(the other Gospels treat his ministry there during only four or
five days at the end of his life). Since Judas knew where to look
for Jesus to hand him over to the authorities, he led a band of
soldiers and officers to the place (vs. 3). The Greek word for
"band" normally meant 600 soldiers, but here it means only a de-
tachment sent by such a "band." The "officers" were from the
Sanhedrin, as is indicated by the reference to "the chief priests
and the Pharisees." The search party took lanterns and torches so
that they could identify Jesus in a dark place, and weapons to
subdue him and his followers if they resisted arrest.

Jesus was fully aware of Judas' treachery and of the plot
against him, but he was ready to meet death to complete his
earthly work, so he came forward (vs. 4); he did not wait in the
shade of the trees for them to hunt him out. Judas had come to
identify Jesus as well as to show the group where to find him.
But Jesus did not wait to be identified; he asked whom they were
seeking, and when they said Jesus of Nazareth, he identified himself (vs. 5); he was ready to accept the Cross. In his calm and
dignity his divine greatness made itself felt, and the arresting
party, temporarily awed, shrank back and fell to the ground (vs.
6). To the Gospel writer this meant that they could not take him
against his will; only by his willing acceptance of the Cross could
men bring him to it.

When Jesus again asked the crowd whom they wanted and received the same answer (vs. 7), he showed that his concern was
not for himself but for his disciples. He willingly surrendered to
his captors, but asked that his followers (Judas was now no longer
his follower) be permitted to depart safely (vs. 8). He knew that
if he was accused of revolt against Rome or treason to his people,
his followers could be arrested and punished with him, but he

asked for their release, and it is implied that they were allowed to go unharmed. Matthew 26:56 and Mark 14:50 say that they fled in panic, but here Jesus, by his forethought and request, saved them from danger and so continued the constant care for them of which 6:39 and 17:12 had spoken. Verse 9 says that he lost none of his followers; this means none except Judas, as 17:12 has already stated.

Whatever failure lay ahead for Simon Peter, he did have courage (vs. 10). In the face of armed soldiers and Jewish officers he drew his sword and cut off the right ear of Malchus, the high priest's slave who had come to assist in the arrest (see also vs. 26). Since a Jew was not supposed to carry a sword during a feast, Peter's act would indicate that the Jewish Passover had not yet begun (compare 18:28); in this Gospel the Last Supper was eaten the evening before the evening of the Passover Feast. Jesus stopped Peter's attempt to defend his Master by force (vs. 11). The cup of suffering that lay ahead was the Father's will which the Son was ready to accept; would Peter want Jesus to refuse to do what the Father had sent him to do?

The Condemnation of Jesus (18:12—19:16)

Jesus Taken to Annas and Caiaphas; Peter's Denial (18:12-27)

The arrest inevitably followed. Jesus willingly surrendered. The soldiers and members of the Jewish Sanhedrin seized and bound him (vs. 12) and led him to the house of Annas in Jerusalem (vs. 13). Annas was not then the high priest, but had been from A.D. 6 to 15, and from the first-century Jewish historian Josephus we learn that four of his sons also held the high priesthood. He was evidently the political leader of the Jewish priestly party, and Caiaphas, the actual high priest (A.D. 18-36), was his son-in-law and under his influence. Caiaphas was high priest "that year" (vs. 13); this means not that there was a new high priest every year, but that in that special year, when Jesus came before the high priest, Caiaphas held the office. But Annas had at least as much power as Caiaphas, so the Gospel can also call Annas the high priest. Verse 14 recalls 11:49-52, where Caiaphas callously says that to preserve peace and protect the priesthood's privileges Jesus should be put to death without regard for legal justice.

But before describing Jesus' trial, the Gospel tells how Peter's courage began to fail. He followed Jesus to the house of the high priest (vs. 15). So did one other disciple. He is not named, but may be the beloved disciple of 13:23. This other disciple may have been of priestly family; at least he knew the household of the priestly leader Annas and, by speaking to the maid at the gateway, was able not only to enter the house himself (vs. 15) but also to get Peter admitted (vs. 16). The maid at the gate, cautious and uncertain, asked Peter if he were a disciple of Jesus. Peter, feeling the danger of his situation in the midst of the servants, soldiers, and officers, denied it (vs. 17). It was a cold spring night, and the group who had gone to the garden to arrest Jesus had made a fire and now stood around it to keep warm. Peter stood with them, concerned for Jesus, unwilling to leave, but afraid to admit boldly who he was (vs. 18).

The high priest in verse 19 is still Annas; not until verse 24 does he send Jesus to Caiaphas. (A Syriac manuscript of the Gospel puts verse 24 after verse 13, and a Greek manuscript puts it after verse 13a; but these are later attempts to change the fact that in this Gospel, Jesus was examined by Annas and not by Caiaphas, the actual high priest.) When Annas asked Jesus about his disciples and teaching (vs. 19), Jesus could say that he had taught openly not only in the synagogues but also in the Temple at Jerusalem, the special place of influence of the priests. So it was wrong to pretend that he had been teaching or plotting in secret; he had taught openly for all the world to hear (vs. 20). He invited Annas to ask others what he had taught (vs. 21); any charge against him should be supported by open testimony.

This bold reply angered an officer standing nearby; the officer thought that Jesus was disrespectful to Annas, and so he slapped Jesus and rebuked him (vs. 22). Jesus challenged his attacker (vs. 23): if Jesus' defense of his open and widely known teaching was in any way wrong, the error should be pointed out; if no error could be pointed out—and Jesus implied that none could—then it was a shameful injustice to strike Jesus for his justifiable protest. Annas, without finding any clear ground for action against Jesus, sent Jesus to Caiaphas for more official action (vs. 24). The hearing before Annas was apparently an unofficial night hearing, held to try to find some solid basis on which the leaders could bring Jesus before Pilate the Roman governor and demand that Pilate execute him.

As Peter stood with the men around the fire in the high

priest's courtyard, they challenged him a second time (the maid at the gate made the first challenge; see vs. 17). Again the Greek indicates uncertainty or hesitation in the question. Peter again denied being a disciple of Jesus (vs. 25). But then one of the group, a relative of Malchus, whose right ear Peter had cut off in the garden (vs. 10), took a good look at Peter and asked more confidently whether he had not seen Peter with Jesus in the garden (vs. 26). Peter again denied it; the cock crowed (vs. 27). What Jesus had foreseen (13:38) had occurred: the strength of Peter was not as great as he had boasted, nor was it equal to the crisis. Only as a forgiven failure could Peter be a leader of the Church.

Jesus Examined and Condemned by Pilate (18:28—19:16)

This Gospel does not report a questioning of Jesus by Caiaphas. Jesus is sent to Caiaphas, kept there until early morning, and then taken to the Praetorium, the governor's residence, to be handed over to Pilate (vs. 28). The Praetorium may have been in the Tower of Antonia, at the northwest corner of the Temple area, but more likely it was in the fortress and castle that had been built by Herod the Great (40-4 B.C.) near the west gate of Jerusalem. This Herodian castle was later used by Roman governors such as Pilate when they came to Jerusalem from Caesarea on the seacoast, which they used as their capital city. Pilate was in Jerusalem because great crowds of pilgrims always came there for the Passover. It was the annual feast which celebrated Israel's liberation from Egypt, raised Jewish hopes of a new deliverance from Rome, and so might spark an uprising which the Roman governor would want to nip in the bud.

The Jewish leaders who brought Jesus to Pilate did not enter the Praetorium. It was a pagan place, and so was unclean for a Jew. Therefore, since the Passover, for which they had to be ceremonially clean, was to be eaten that night, they refused to enter and stayed outside (vs. 28). The irony of this was that they were scrupulously careful about ceremonial cleanness but indifferent to justice and the claim of the Son of God. Pilate had to go out to talk to them—the first stage in his being forced to yield to the will of the Jewish leaders (vs. 29). When he asked what charge they made against Jesus, their haughty attitude was still more evident; they merely stated that if Jesus had not been an evildoer they would not have brought him to Pilate for punishment (vs. 30). Pilate perhaps was fully aware of what they wanted, since verses 3 and 12 seem to mean that Roman soldiers had taken part in the arrest, and he knew that they wanted him to inflict the death penalty on Jesus. So he tauntingly told them to take Jesus and punish him themselves (vs. 31). Since they wanted the death penalty and under Rome's rule had no right to inflict it, they had to say what they wanted and insist that Pilate pronounce the judgment. Had they executed Jesus, they would have done so by stoning on a charge of blasphemy (Lev. 24:16). Jesus had spoken of being lifted up, and thus referred to death on the cross. In this inability of the Jews to execute him and this necessity to get Pilate to do so by the Roman method of crucifixion, the Gospel writer sees new proof of Jesus' foreknowledge (vs. 32); he knew by what manner he would be put to death and so had spoken, as in 3:14; 8:28; 12:32-34, of being "lifted up."

The Gospel does not state the charge which the Jewish leaders had made against Jesus, but when Pilate went back into the Praetorium to question Jesus, he asked him whether he was the King of the Jews (vs. 33). This implies that the Jewish leaders had reported to Pilate Jesus' claim to be the Messiah of the Jews, and had interpreted it as a political claim to kingship and so as a proof that Jesus was plotting revolt against Rome. The Messiah, according to usual Jewish thought, was expected to be the king of his people, and so this claim of Jesus, while here distorted, could plausibly be interpreted as rebellion against Roman rule and therefore as a crime that Pilate must punish. (See the same distortion of Jesus' Messianic claim in Luke 23:2.) Since Jesus was hailed as King of Israel on his triumphal entrance into Jerusalem (12:13-15), the charge could seem plausible and Pilate could have heard of it.

Jesus inquired whether Pilate asked because he thought the charge was justified, or whether he was only repeating what others had charged (vs. 34). Pilate impatiently refused to get into what he considered merely an exasperating Jewish dispute (vs. 35). The Jewish leaders had handed Jesus over to him; Jesus must have done something to antagonize them; what had he done? In his reply (vs. 36) Jesus accepted the title of king; properly understood, he was a king; in fact, he was *the* King, rightly claiming full obedience from all men. But he was not the kind of king Pilate had in mind. Had he been a king with political and military ambition and methods, his followers would have fought to resist his arrest. But he had renounced such use of force (vs. 11). His kingship did not owe its origin or authority to this world; it was an authority given him by the Father and was to be exercised in such a way that without the use of force or political power—in fact, by suffering—he would prove to be the Savior of the world and the Lord of all who believe.

Pilate did not understand Jesus, but he perceived that in some sense Jesus was accepting the title of king, so he pushed his question: "So you are a king?" Jesus accepted the title, but at once moved from the idea of political kingship, which Pilate could understand, to the idea of a kingdom of truth in which every person who responds to divine truth and commits himself to it would listen to him and obey him (vs. 37). It is a kingdom of obedience to God's will as made known by Jesus, a kingdom where God is truly made known, accepted as Lord, and obeyed. Pilate made a short, impatient reply (vs. 38): "What is truth?" Perhaps the question was cynical: Who can tell what the truth is? Men do not know how to find it. Or perhaps the question was scornful: You are on trial for your life, and yet you are idly talking about what truth is. Why not quit this idle discussion and think how to save your life? In either case, Pilate saw no danger in Jesus and no use of talking further with him.

Going out of the Praetorium, Pilate told the Jewish leaders and crowd that he found no crime in Jesus that deserved punishment (vs. 38). This is the first of three statements by Pilate that Jesus had done nothing that deserved condemnation (see also 19:4, 6). But instead of releasing Jesus, as justice would have required, he tried to get the Jews to ask for Jesus' release (vs. 39). Because he needed to get along with the Jewish leaders and did not want to antagonize them, he tried to win them to some compromise by which he could let Jesus go. He recalled his custom—not known from any first-century source outside the Gospels, but no doubt used to pacify the Jewish crowds present at Passover—of releasing each Passover one prisoner whom the Jews requested. He suggested that they let him release Jesus at this Passover, and to stir up their nationalist pride he referred to Jesus as the King of the Jews. Surely they would not want it said that he had executed their King! Then let them agree that he release this King. But they rejected his proposal (vs. 40). They intended to get Jesus condemned, so they promptly asked for the release of another prisoner. This was Barabbas, called "a robber," that is, a brig-

and who lived by robbery and plunder and who by this law-
less life aimed to make as much trouble as possible for the Roman governor. By asking for Barabbas they showed their hatred
of Roman rule and also kept Pilate from releasing Jesus. It is implied, but not said, that Pilate did release Barabbas.

Pilate then tried another scheme. He had Jesus scourged
(19:1), in the hope that the sight of the bleeding and suffering
prisoner would appease the Jewish leaders and make them willing
for him to let Jesus go free. The Roman soldiers who had the task
of flogging Jesus shared Pilate's contempt for Jesus' claim to be
a king. In mockery they made him a painful crown from a thorny
plant and put it on his head; they put on him a purple robe such
as kings wear (vs. 2); in contemptuous sport they hailed him as
King of the Jews; their scorn and contempt showed openly when
they slapped him with coarse brutality (vs. 3). In the other Gospels these acts follow Jesus' condemnation; here they are done to
try to satisfy the Jews without actually condemning Jesus to death.

The flogging completed, Pilate brought Jesus out of the Praetorium, where the mocking had taken place, so that the accusers
could see Jesus in his mock robes of royalty and with his bleeding
back and head. He repeated that he had found no crime in Jesus,
and hoped that Jesus would seem so ridiculous a figure—obviously no king—that none would object to his release (vs. 4).
"Here is the man!" (vs. 5) meant: Look at this mocked, bleeding,
and obviously helpless fellow; he is no king, no danger to Rome;
why not let me release him? But the leaders cried out for Jesus'
crucifixion (vs. 6). This was the first time they made this specific
demand; they were pressing Pilate for action.

Pilate, saying the third time that he found no crime in Jesus,
told them impatiently to take Jesus and crucify him; he did not
want to crucify an innocent man. He knew, and they knew, that
they had no right to crucify Jesus; perhaps he said this to make
the accusers realize that they did not control him and had to accept his decision. But they had a new point. Dropping for the
moment the charge that by claiming to be the political king of the
Jews he was a rebel against Rome, they charged that he had
violated their law against blasphemy (Lev. 24:16). He had
claimed to be the Son of God, and for this blasphemous claim he
deserved to die (vs. 7).

Pilate was already uneasy about Jesus; he sensed in him a power
and nature that puzzled him and made him a little fearful. When

he heard this claim to divine nature and power, he became still more uneasy (vs. 8). Taking Jesus back into the Praetorium so that he could question him privately, he asked Jesus where he came from (vs. 9). He was not asking in what town Jesus had lived; he wanted to know whether Jesus was an ordinary man or had a divine origin. Jesus did not answer; a real answer would have gone far beyond the political realm in which Pilate had any authority to judge him. But because Jesus was conscious of being the Son of God, he would not deny that the title applied to him.

Pilate again was impatient (vs. 10). He had power to execute or release Jesus, and yet Jesus did not answer or seem respectful. Jesus knew that whatever power Pilate had came not from the Emperor Tiberius in Rome but from above, from God (vs. 11). And because the gift of God gave Pilate his power to rule, it was the more terrible that he was about to misuse that divinely given power to execute an innocent man and crucify the Son of God. And for Caiaphas to deliver Jesus to Pilate and use Pilate to get Jesus executed meant that Caiaphas had still greater sin.

Verse 12 indicates that Pilate again went out to the Jewish leaders and tried once more to win their consent to release Jesus. Pilate could have released him at any time after he had found that Jesus had done nothing criminal (18:38). But the Jewish leaders then used their strongest argument. They threatened to tell the emperor in Rome that Pilate had been lenient with a rebel against Rome. That would have hurt Pilate's standing with the emperor. His interest in justice was too weak to control his selfish personal interest. He wanted to be known as Caesar's friend; he dared not seem to tolerate a provincial rebel, said to claim to be king of Palestine. So he had Jesus brought out of the Praetorium, and he himself sat down on the judgment seat to pronounce judgment (vs. 13); he had decided to sentence Jesus to death. The judgment seat was located on a place called "The Pavement," or "Gabbatha" in Aramaic (as "Hebrew" means here); perhaps it was a mosaic pavement.

For this memorable event the Gospel gives the day and hour (vs. 14); Pilate pronounced the sentence at noon (the sixth hour) on the Day of Preparation for the Passover, which, as 18:28 shows, was to be celebrated that evening, when the new day began; the day of the week on which Pilate pronounced sentence was Friday (see vs. 31). Mark 15:25 places the sentence before the third hour, on the morning after the Passover. In the Gospel of John,

Jesus died as the Lamb of God (1:29) at the very time when the Passover lambs were being slain and prepared for the feast.

Since the Jews insisted that Jesus must die for claiming kingship—a claim true in a sense that they did not realize (18:36-37) —Pilate, before passing sentence, taunted them and showed his contempt for Jesus by saying, Here is your supposed King! (vs. 14). Enraged by his taunt, they cried out fiercely for the crucifixion of Jesus. Pilate mockingly replied, "Shall I crucify your King?" With complete disregard of the ancestral Jewish conviction that God is the real King of Israel, the chief priests answered that they had no king but Caesar (vs. 15). They disowned their ancestral faith in their eagerness to get Jesus crucified. Then Pilate handed Jesus over to them to be crucified (vs. 16).

Pilate's act does not mean that the Jewish leaders actually nailed Jesus to the cross, for it is clear from verse 31 that the soldiers of verse 23 were Roman soldiers, under Pilate's authority. What verse 16 means is that the execution of Jesus resulted from the condemnation that the Jewish leaders sought. We cannot acquit either Pilate or the Jewish leaders of blame for the death of Jesus. But we cannot blame the entire Jewish people of that day for a wrong of which few of them knew and many of these disapproved, and we cannot blame later members of that people for an act of which they do not approve.

The King of the Jews Crucified and Buried (19:17-42)

The Crucifixion of Jesus (19:17-23)

The crucifixion story is told in simple language. Jesus was taken outside the city (vs. 17). In the procession he carried his own cross (or the crossbar, which condemned criminals were usually required to carry). He was crucified at "the place of a skull," or in Aramaic (as "Hebrew" means here) "Golgotha." Was the place a skull-shaped hillock? Or had a skull from an ancient burial been found there and so given the place its name? We do not know. With Jesus, the soldiers crucified also two condemned criminals who had been awaiting execution (vs. 18). That Jesus was placed in the center, between these two, symbolized to the Gospel writer the central role of Jesus in God's redemptive work.

It seems to have been customary to write on a placard the accusation for which the person was being executed, and to nail the placard to the cross above the head of the condemned person. Pilate had a placard written giving the name of Jesus, his home city of Nazareth, and the charge against him: he had claimed to be "the King of the Jews" (vs. 19). In other words, Jesus was executed on the pretense that he was a political revolutionary trying to become king of the Jews in Palestine. Only by giving this misleading political turn to Jesus' Messiahship could Pilate even try to justify his execution of Jesus, in whom he had found no crime.

The place of execution was near Jerusalem (vs. 20); traditionally it was where the Church of the Holy Sepulcher now stands in Jerusalem, and this may possibly be the actual site. Apparently it was close to a road, for many Jews passed by and read the placard on the cross. Pilate had made it easy for all to read by writing the charge not only in Latin, the official language of Rome, but also in the two languages which Jews then spoke, Greek and Aramaic (as "Hebrew" probably means here).

The chief priests disliked the wording; it sounded as if the Jews had wanted Jesus to be their King. So they asked Pilate to change the title to say that Jesus *claimed* to be King of the Jews (vs. 21). Pilate refused to change what he had written (vs. 22); in this the Gospel writer sees a hint that regardless of Jesus' rejection by his own people, he was in fact the rightful King of Israel (1:49; 12:13, 15).

The Contrast of Callousness and Love (19:24-27)

The soldiers who executed a criminal could take his garments as bonus pay for their work. Evidently four soldiers had been sent to execute Jesus and the two criminals. They each took a share of Jesus' garments, but since his tunic, woven in one continuous piece, would be of no use to any of the soldiers if they tore it into four pieces, they agreed to draw lots to see which one would get it (vss. 23-24). In this the writer sees the fulfillment of Psalm 22:18. This Psalm was much used in the Apostolic Church as having been a poetic forecast of the suffering of Jesus. That this Psalm spoke of just such a drawing of lots as the soldiers made indicated to the Gospel writer and to the Church that Jesus' suffering had a constructive place in God's plan.

Almost all of Jesus' followers were absent, fearful that the hostility against Jesus would strike them also. But a few loyal women and one loyal man stood near the cross, giving Jesus whatever comfort their presence could afford (vs. 25). It seems that there were four women, named in two pairs; to take "his mother's sister" to be the same as "Mary the wife of Clopas" would give two sisters named Mary, which to say the least seems extremely unlikely. For hints that the mother of Jesus had more understanding of his ministry than the other Gospels suggest, see 2:3-5, 12. The "Clopas" mentioned may be the "Cleopas" of Luke 24:18. "Mary Magdalene" means "Mary of Magdala," a town on the western shore of the Sea of Galilee (compare Luke 8:2, which many connect with the sinful woman of Luke 7:37). On the help that women gave to Jesus and his disciples during his ministry, see Luke 8:3.

In John 19:25-27 the attention centers almost entirely on Mary the mother of Jesus. Jesus wanted her to be cared for after his death. The "disciple whom he loved" (vs. 26; 13:23) stood near, with the women; here, as in the case of the "other disciple" of 18:15-16, this disciple was free to go safely to places where the other disciples would be in danger; he had friends in high places in Jerusalem. Does this fit John the son of Zebedee, the Galilean fisherman? Or Lazarus of Bethany, a suburb of Jerusalem? (See the Introduction.) Speaking to his mother first (vs. 26), Jesus called her not "Mother" but "Lady." ("Woman" sounds a bit disrespectful to modern ears, and the Greek word does not have a disrespectful tone.) He tells her to regard the beloved disciple henceforth as her son. Similarly, he tells the beloved disciple to treat Mary henceforth as though she were his own mother (vs. 27). In obedience to this trust, the beloved disciple at once took her to his own home. This naturally suggests that his home was in or near Jerusalem; this would fit Lazarus of Bethany better than it would John the son of Zebedee, who lived in Galilee. (The statement that John had a second home in Jerusalem is only an inference from this passage; no independent evidence supports it. If John was the beloved disciple, the passage means that he at once took Mary to his *temporary* residence where he was staying in Jerusalem during the Passover Feast.)

The Death of Jesus (19:28-37)

With his mother cared for, Jesus could feel that he had done all he had been sent to do and had cared for his own as fully as possible. Death was near. But thirst was intense, and he said so (vs. 28). In this the writer sees one more indication that God's plan included the Cross, since he found this incident forecast in Scripture (Pss. 22:15; 69:21). A bowl full of sour wine (this is what "vinegar" means) was at hand. Perhaps the soldiers had brought it to drink while they watched the executed men die. "They" (probably the soldiers) put a sponge in the wine, and putting the sponge on hyssop they reached it up for Jesus to suck wine from the sponge (vs. 29). Since hyssop was not a stiff-stemmed plant, some interpreters think that the Greek word for "hyssop" is a copyist's mistake for a similar-sounding Greek word for "lance," which a soldier would have and could use to hold a sponge up to Jesus' mouth as he hung on the cross. But perhaps hyssop was used, and the Gospel writer, remembering Exodus 12:22, mentions it to recall that Jesus was the true Passover Lamb, as I Corinthians 5:7 also suggests. This is the one act of kindness to Jesus reported in the Crucifixion story.

In his final word Jesus declared that his earthly life and work were finished; then he bowed his head to accept the death he had known was God's will (vs. 30).

Jesus died on Friday afternoon. The Sabbath would begin at sundown. As Deuteronomy 21:22-23 shows, the Law forbade leaving an executed criminal hanging on the cross overnight; and it would violate the Sabbath to take the bodies down during the Sabbath. So the Jews asked Pilate, the authority in charge, to have the soldiers break the legs of the crucified men to hasten their death, so that their bodies could be taken down before sundown, when the Sabbath would begin (vs. 31). At Pilate's command the soldiers broke the legs of the other two men (vs. 32), but since Jesus was already dead, they did not need to treat him so (vs. 33). But one soldier, no doubt in idle, callous play, pierced Jesus' side with the lance he carried (vs. 34).

The fact that blood and water flowed from the wound was obviously of great importance for the Gospel writer; in verse 35 he insists that a trustworthy eyewitness reported this. Is the writer claiming to be the eyewitness? Possibly he is. At the very least he claims that he writes on the authority of a trustworthy eyewitness, whose testimony aimed to lead others—including the readers and hearers of the Gospel—to believe and so be saved. To what do "blood and water" refer? Some say that the blood and water indicate merely that death had actually taken place and the heart had ruptured; Jesus really died for men. Others say that the words refer to the two sacraments, the Lord's Supper, represented by the blood, and Baptism, represented by the water; I John 5:6-8 seems to support this. But in this Gospel, blood and water represent the giving of life (3:5; 6:53-56). More likely, while a reference to the two sacraments is probably included, the Gospel sees symbolized here the entire life-giving effect of Jesus' death, and this central meaning of his work is underlined by the emphatic eyewitness assurance of verse 35.

Verse 36 emphasizes the fact that this event, like other key events in Jesus' life, was forecast in Scripture. As was required of the Passover lamb, no bone of Jesus was broken (Exod. 12:46; Num. 9:12); in this Gospel, Jesus dies when the Passover lambs are being slain and prepared for the Passover Feast. He is the true Passover Lamb (I Cor. 5:7), and dies to take away men's sins (1:29). The piercing of Jesus' side is reported as a fulfillment of Zechariah 12:10, quoted according to the original Hebrew (vs. 37).

Jesus' Body Receives Honorable Burial (19:38-42)

Two prominent Jewish leaders buried Jesus. Joseph of Arimathea (a town about twenty-two miles northwest of Jerusalem) took the lead (vs. 38). He believed in Jesus—this Gospel alone says this about him—but had been afraid to confess it openly because of the official Jewish disapproval of Jesus (12:42-43 criticizes such secret faith because it lets men's praise or blame rule life). Now Joseph plucked up courage and got permission from Pilate to take the body of Jesus. During the burial he was helped by Nicodemus (vs. 39; see 3:1-9; 7:50-52), who is not called a believer in Jesus, but whose act here suggests that he had become one. He must have been a man of means, for a hundred pounds (this pound contained twelve ounces) of myrrh and aloes was a costly, lavish gift. In the other Gospels, Jesus' body was buried hastily and without adequate preparation according to Jewish standards; here that ministry of love was performed with rich devotion befitting the unique One who had died (vs. 40).

It was almost time for the Sabbath and Passover to begin; before sundown the burial had to be completed. There was no time to carry the body far. Near at hand was a garden in which was a new tomb, hewn out of the rock (vs. 41). Such an unused tomb, the writer implies, was suitable for the Christ's burial. It is not said whether Joseph owned the tomb; but it was near, and so they laid the body there just before the going down of the sun on that Good Friday marked the beginning of the Sabbath (vs. 42).

The Resurrection and the Gift of the Holy Spirit
(20:1-29)

The Empty Tomb (20:1-10)

The Gospel implies, but does not clearly say, that the scriptural command to rest on the Sabbath kept the disciples from visiting the tomb. But they knew where it was; Mary Magdalene (vs. 1) and Peter and the beloved disciple (vs. 3) knew where to go. None of them went to the tomb until early Sunday morning. While the Sabbath had ended at sundown on Saturday, the night was not a good time to visit the tomb. But the eagerness of Mary Magdalene is indicated by the fact that she came to it early Sunday morning, while it was still dark. She saw that the stone which Joseph and Nicodemus had placed against the entrance (they must have done this, though 19:42 does not say so) had been removed. Thinking, as verse 2 shows, that someone had taken the body to some unknown place, she ran and told Simon Peter and the beloved disciple.

These two men ran to the tomb (vss. 3-4). The beloved disciple, probably the younger, outran Peter, reached the open tomb, looked in, and saw that the body was gone but that the linen cloths lay there. (This was a sign of resurrection; had someone taken the body elsewhere, the cloths wrapped around the body would have been carried away too.) In awe he did not enter the tomb (vs. 5). Simon Peter, on arriving, was bolder; as soon as he reached the tomb, he entered it, and saw not only the linen cloths which the beloved disciple had noticed, but also the head-band, neatly rolled up in a place by itself (vss. 6-7). This means either that Jesus had removed it and rolled it up, or, more likely, that in rising from the dead he had simply left the napkin lying where his head had been; as he could appear in a room with closed doors (vss. 19, 26), he could move out of the cloths and napkin without disturbing them.

Peter, it is implied, saw these things without really under-standing what had happened. But the beloved disciple, when he followed Peter into the tomb, "saw and believed" (vs. 8). He realized that Jesus had risen from the dead. Verse 9 states that

these men had not yet realized that the Scriptures, rightly understood, pointed to Jesus' resurrection; as 2:22 and 12:16 say, it
was only after his resurrection that they came to understand
much of what the Scripture meant. But now, with the beloved disciple leading the way, they at least grasped the fact that Jesus had
risen; they began to realize that he was their living Lord (vs. 28).
However, they went away without seeing him (vs. 10).

Jesus Appears to Mary Magdalene (20:11-18)

It was Mary Magdalene who first saw and recognized the risen
Jesus. After running to report that the tomb was open and so
presumably empty, she evidently had returned to it, though more
slowly than the two men. She was weeping at the tomb entrance
(vs. 11); she still thought that Jesus was dead and that someone
had taken away his body. Stooping and looking into the tomb, she
saw two angels, dressed, as angels were reputed to be, in white (vs.
12). They sat near where the head and feet of Jesus had lain
(indicated probably by the position of the linen cloths). They
asked why she was weeping, when evidence of the Resurrection
fact was before her. She replied in words like those she had
spoken to Peter and the beloved disciple (vs. 2); she still thought
that strangers, perhaps enemies, had taken away Jesus' body (vs.
13). The angels play no further part in the story.

Mary turned away, and Jesus stood before her, but she did not
recognize him (vs. 14; see Matt. 28:17; Luke 24:16). He, too,
asked why she wept, when the cause of joy stood before her; and
he added, to draw her attention to him, "Whom do you seek?"
(vs. 15). Still the prisoner of her theory that someone had taken
away the dead body, she could not recognize the risen Jesus but
thought he must be the caretaker of the garden in which she
stood (19:41). If such a one had considered the burial of Jesus
in the garden an intrusion, and so had removed the body, she was
ready to take the body away and give it proper burial if the
gardener would only tell her where he had put it.

Then, as she turned from him, perhaps to look at the tomb
again, she heard him speak her name (see 10:3) and knew who
he was (vs. 16). Turning back in a quick rush of recognition and
joy, she called him "Rabboni"; the "Hebrew" (that is, Aramaic)
word means "My Teacher!" or "My Master!" In her joy at seeing
him she evidently reached out in eager desire to touch him and
know for certain that it was really Jesus. But he stopped her (vs.

17); she must not touch or hold him. He had not returned to resume his former way of life with his disciples in an earthly body. Since he had not yet ascended to the Father, he could appear to her and assure her of his life and presence, but he would no longer live the daily physical life of the earthly ministry.

Mary must go and tell the disciples, assumed to be still in or near Jerusalem, that Jesus was alive and was ascending to the Father, his Father and theirs, his God and theirs. He and they could both speak of God as their Father or God, but the way Jesus here referred to the Father showed that his relation to the Father was different from theirs; as the eternal Son of God, now raised from the dead, he was not related to the Father in the same way that redeemed and mortal men are. That he was alive and ascending to the Father, however, should reassure them and make them know that blessing for them would result (compare 14:18; 16:7).

Mary Magdalene found the disciples (verses 19 and 26 indicate that they had a definite place to stay in or near Jerusalem) and reported that she had seen Jesus and talked with him (vs. 18). Whether they believed her is not said; at least they were prepared for Jesus' appearance to them that evening.

Jesus Gives the Spirit to His Disciples (20:19-23)

On the evening of the Resurrection day the disciples were gathered behind locked doors (vs. 19); they feared that the people who brought about Jesus' death would try to kill his chief followers. Jesus, not stopped by walls and doors, suddenly appeared in their midst; he could make himself seen and heard by believers, although we cannot explain how. Greeting them with the traditional Jewish greeting, "Peace be with you," he showed them his hands, pierced by nails when nailed to the cross, and his side, pierced by the soldier's lance (19:34); this was to remove all doubt as to who he was. How this spiritual body could show the marks of the physical harm done him on the cross is not explained. It was the same body, but changed to be the form suitable to his new life and relations with his disciples. Prepared by the report of Mary Magdalene and convinced by seeing the marks of his crucifixion, they were gladdened by his presence (vs. 20).

But Jesus had come not merely to give them personal assurance, but also to send them into the world to carry forward his work. The Father, as this Gospel has said many times, had sent him into the world, and he had faithfully done what he had been sent to do; now he sent the disciples into the world to announce and continue his work (vs. 21). But they could not do this work in their own strength. As he had promised them (15:26; 16:7), he now gave them the Holy Spirit (vs. 22) to bear witness to him, to remind them of his words and work, to teach them new truth, and to be with them in their work for him. (In Acts 2:4 the Spirit is given about seven weeks later, on Pentecost.)

As the disciples witness and work by the guidance and power of the Holy Spirit, they can announce with certainty the forgiveness of sin whereby they find repentance and faith, and can also announce the continuance of sin and guilt in those who do not respond in faith to the message of God's love in Christ (vs. 23). This is no promise of official power which leaders may exercise regardless of whether they are personally true and loyal to Christ; only as Spirit-filled and Spirit-guided men may they thus speak for him with authority, but as Spirit-guided men they need not hesitate to speak and act with assurance.

Jesus Appears to Thomas Also (20:24-29)

Thomas, cautious, inclined to be skeptical, but loyal as far as his understanding went, was not with the other disciples on that Resurrection evening (vs. 24). His name "Didymus" means "Twin," but the New Testament never says who his twin brother or sister was, nor whether his twin was a disciple. When told that the others had seen the risen Lord, he refused to believe it unless he not only saw the nail prints but even touched these prints and the wound in Jesus' side (vs. 25). Jesus had shown the nail prints and side wound to the other disciples (vs. 20); in wanting to *see* the prints Thomas did not ask more than the others had already been given, but he also wanted to touch them—he thought in terms of a strictly physical resurrection.

The next Sunday (vs. 26) the disciples were again behind locked doors in the place where they were staying. This time Thomas was with them. (Perhaps the reference to these two Sunday appearances is meant to help to justify the later church practice of observing Sunday as the day of the Resurrection; compare I Cor. 16:2; Rev. 1:10.) Jesus, unhindered by solid walls and doors, again appeared in their midst and greeted them as before (vs. 26; see vs. 19). Then he offered to meet the test which Thomas had proposed (vs. 25), and added in appeal and warning, "Do not be faithless, but believing" (vs. 27). Thomas faced an opportunity for immeasurable privilege and blessing, but to fail to believe would be an unspeakable catastrophe. This is what this Gospel keeps saying: faith is the key to life; unbelief leads to death and ruin.

Thomas rose to his opportunity. It is not said whether he touched Jesus; apparently he did not need to do that. He saw and recognized the risen Jesus, and the stubborn skeptic, now convinced, gives the Gospel's climactic confession of faith—this risen Jesus is his Lord and his God (vs. 28; see 1:1). This is one form of the full confession which the Gospel was written to lead men to make. Verse 31 states it in another way, not meant to be different in content: the risen Jesus is the Christ, the Son of God, the risen Lord and Master of his disciples; to every believer he is the divine Savior of the world, God present with his people to save them and give them eternal life. ·

Verse 29 gives Thomas a mild rebuke for being unwilling to believe without visible proof that Jesus had risen. The purpose of these words, however, is not so much to criticize Thomas as to point forward to the multitudes who in the days of the Gospel writer and in later days believe and make the same confession, without requiring such visible proof. The rich blessing of God will rest on all such believers in Christ.

THE PURPOSE OF THE GOSPEL
John 20:30-31

The original draft of the Gospel, it seems, ended with the conclusion in verses 30-31. Chapter 21 was thus a later addition or appendix. Verse 30 assures the reader that Jesus did many other signs besides those this Gospel contains. This statement, following so closely the Resurrection appearances just reported, implies that they, like the miracles told earlier, were signs of God's presence and power at work in Jesus for the salvation of men. For the purpose of the Gospel there was no need to tell every sign the disciples could remember; a selection could carry the essential message and achieve the writer's purpose. He states that purpose clearly (vs. 31). He has written to lead the readers and hearers of the Gospel—and he thinks especially of those already Christian—to believe in a deep, true, and full sense. The heart of what they need to believe is that Jesus is the Christ, the Son of God. The writer is convinced that a right understanding of the person and work of Jesus is essential to a mature and saving faith. The gift of God to those who thus believe is life, eternal life. It is given to them in the name of Christ—that is, in their grateful believing relationship to Jesus as he has made himself known to them.

Thus the Gospel was written to make clear (1) what God wants of men—they should believe; (2) who Jesus was and is—he fulfills the promises of God to the Jews and is the divine Son of God; and (3) what God gives to those who believe—eternal life beginning now and lasting forever.

ANOTHER RESURRECTION APPEARANCE

John 21:1-25

Chapters 1-20 would form a complete Gospel, and 20:30-31 is a perfect conclusion for the Gospel. Chapter 21 seems to be a later addition (even though it is found in all complete early manuscripts of this Gospel). Why was it added? Not merely to report another Resurrection appearance (vss. 1-14); chapter 20 had already told enough to make it clear that Jesus had risen and was the living divine Lord of the true believer. Two other reasons seem more vital: to tell how Jesus commissioned Peter as shepherd of Christ's flock (vss. 15-19), and to correct a misunderstanding of what Jesus had said about the beloved disciple (vss. 20-23).

The Third Appearance to the Disciples (21:1-14)

The three Resurrection appearances in chapter 20—one to Mary Magdalene near the tomb and two to the disciples in the closed room—took place in or near Jerusalem. The third appearance to the disciples (21:14) occurred on the shore of the Sea of Tiberias (this name for the Sea of Galilee came into use by the latter part of the first century A.D.). The disciples, it is implied, had returned to Galilee after the two Jerusalem appearances of the risen Lord. Seven disciples were together (vs. 2). Simon Peter, Thomas, and Nathanael have been mentioned before in this Gospel; the sons of Zebedee are mentioned only here, and are not named individually; the other two disciples present are not identified at all.

Peter, who had been a fisherman before following Jesus, announced that he intended to go fishing. This need not mean that he had given up his faith in Jesus and had decided to go back to fishing for a living; it may mean only that he and his friends needed food, and since they had a boat (vs. 3), he decided to catch fish for their needs. The others went with him. They set out at evening, and during the night hours caught nothing.

At daybreak the disciples saw Jesus standing on the shore, but they, like Mary Magdalene (20:14), did not recognize him (vs. 4). The dimness of the light at early dawn may have given them a partial excuse. He called them "children" (or "lads") and asked whether they had caught anything for food (vs. 5). When they said, "No," he told them to cast their net on the right side of the boat (vs. 6). They obeyed and made so large a catch that they could not haul in the net. This was a "sign" to the beloved disciple; just as in 20:8 he was the first to believe, so now he first discerned that it was the Lord standing on the shore and directing them in this remarkable catch. When he told Peter that it was the risen Lord (vs. 7), Peter, always quick to act, put on his outer garment, which he had stripped off for the work of sailing and fishing, and jumped into the lake and swam to shore (vs. 8). The rest of the disciples came more slowly, bringing the boat and pulling the net along for the last two hundred cubits, that is, three hundred feet, until they touched shore and could disembark. (A cubit was 18 inches.)

On the shore they saw a fire burning—presumably made by Jesus—and on it a fish (or several fish?); baking on the fire or lying nearby was bread (vs. 9). It was a meal of fish and bread such as 6:1-13 reports. Verse 10 seems to suggest that the fish on the coals was not enough to feed the entire group, so Jesus had Peter bring some of the remarkable catch they had just made under his guidance. Peter hauled the net to shore, and found in it 153 fish (vs. 11). Some have found a deep meaning in this number; it is said that this was the total number of the kinds of fish known at that time, and so it signifies the universality of the gospel, which is to be preached to all men; the disciples as "fishers of men" are to bring men of all races and nations into the Church. But the number may refer only to the actual count of a great catch of fish. That so many fish did not tear the net seems to be regarded as a remarkable and perhaps miraculous thing, just as the catch of the fish at Jesus' command was considered a miracle.

With adequate food provided, Jesus called the disciples to eat (vs. 12). They knew it was Jesus the risen Lord, but in awe did not dare to question him. Jesus acted as host and gave them first the bread and then the fish (vs. 13). Much of the meal he had provided directly; some of the fish he had provided by directing his disciples in their fishing. All this food was in one way or another his provision for their needs. The center of Jesus' third appearance to them (vs. 14) was a common meal, but it is not said that Jesus ate of it.

Peter's Ministry and Martyrdom (21:15-19)

Verses 15-23 tell what Jesus said as to what lay ahead for the two leading disciples. In this Gospel, Simon Peter has been prominent throughout, and the beloved disciple, after his first mention in 13:23, has taken a place of remarkable prominence; indeed, if he was Lazarus, he has been prominent from chapter 11 on. Jesus after his resurrection said something about the future of both Peter and the beloved disciple.

He spoke first to Peter. In a way that recalled the threefold denial of Jesus by Peter, Jesus three times asked Peter whether he loved him, and Peter three times replied that he did (vss. 15-17). Each time Peter added that Jesus, who knew all things (vs. 17), knew that Peter loved him. In this passage the Gospel uses two Greek verbs which mean "to love": it is often said that one of these verbs means a higher, more spiritual love, while the other refers to a warm human liking and affection which is not base or cheap but is not so noble or high as the love meant by the first. But this Gospel uses the two verbs without indicating any difference in meaning between them. It uses both verbs in speaking of Jesus' love for Lazarus (ch. 11), and in speaking of his love for the beloved disciple (from 13:23 on). It uses both of these verbs to describe God's love for man, the Father's love for the Son, Jesus' love for men, men's love for other men, and men's love for Jesus. This Gospel thus makes no difference between the two verbs; both refer to a worthy love. Jesus asked Peter whether he had such love for his Master, and Peter protested that, in spite of his shameful denial of Jesus, he did. Similarly, we need not make any real distinction between "feed my lambs," "tend my sheep," and "feed my sheep." The point is that Jesus three times instructed Peter to be a pastor to the flock of Christ. Thus Peter was restored to his position as the prominent leader of the group of disciples and was given a charge to be a faithful shepherd of the Christian group.

Then Jesus foretold the martyrdom of Peter, to come in old age (vss. 18-19). His death was to be a martyr's death; his accepting of that martyr death would bring glory to God by showing Peter's faith and loyalty to Christ. Verse 18 is not explicit, but it seems to hint that Peter's arms would be stretched out (on a cross) for his execution. (The later tradition that he was crucified head downward goes beyond what this passage says.)

After speaking of Peter's future role as pastor and of his final witness to Christ by martyrdom, Jesus then said, "Follow me." It seems from verse 20 that this meant that Peter was to come aside with Jesus for some unexplained purpose, but probably for the Gospel writer the command also included Peter's lifelong following of Jesus.

The Role of the Beloved Disciple (21:20-24)

As Jesus and Peter walked away, Peter, always quick to note and comment on what was happening, saw the beloved disciple following them (vs. 20). He was following his Lord without being asked to do so. Peter asked Jesus what was to happen to that disciple (vs. 21). Jesus did not tell Peter what would happen to the man; he only said that if he wanted the beloved disciple to remain alive and continue in the Church until he returned at the end of this age, that would not be a matter for Peter to know or decide (vs. 22). Peter's one task was to follow Jesus and fulfill his own responsibility to Jesus; he was to be pastor of the flock, faithful until in old age he became a martyr for his Master. The future of the beloved disciple was Jesus' concern; it was nothing which Peter needed to know.

This saying was remembered in the Church, but was misunderstood (vs. 23). It was taken to mean that Jesus had promised that this beloved disciple would not die but would live until the Lord returned. This could be a natural inference if this beloved disciple was Lazarus; he had already died and had been raised (see ch. 11), and Christians might easily believe that he would not have to die again. Probably this beloved disciple had died by the time chapter 21 was written, and Christians were troubled by the idea that Jesus had promised something which had not been fulfilled; Jesus was thought to have promised that this disciple would not die, but he had died.

The writer corrects this misunderstanding. He points out that Jesus made no such definite promise; he only told Peter that the future lot of the beloved disciple was a matter that Peter did not need to understand. The beloved disciple might live until Jesus returned, but Jesus did not say whether he would or not. What counts for each disciple is to fulfill his own task and give his witness to Christ.

This beloved disciple is then named as the witness and in some sense the writer of this Gospel (vs. 24). Two things permit us to think that he may not have written the book with his own hand. One is that the use of scribes or assistants in writing was widely known in ancient times; a person could be responsible for the basic content of a book without doing the actual composition of the sentences. The other is that in this verse we read that "we know that his testimony is true." Certainly the words "we" and "his" show that someone other than the beloved disciple is speaking. At least in this verse, probably in all of chapter 21, and perhaps throughout the Gospel, someone other than the beloved disciple is writing down the witness of that disciple. The man who wrote this verse belongs to the Christian group who remember and hand on the witness of that disciple. They earnestly state that the testimony they give in the name of the beloved disciple is true and dependable.

Conclusion (21:25)

The conclusion in verse 25 is less significant than the conclusion which 20:30-31 gives to the original draft of the Gospel. The writer simply says that Jesus had done many more things than are here recorded; even in adding chapter 21 he had no idea of telling all of Jesus' acts that he remembered. Speaking with literary exaggeration, the writer says that the world could not contain all the books that would have to be written to record all of the available tradition.

Verse 25 is a good reminder; our Gospels were not intended to be complete lives of Jesus. They tell what the writers con sidered essential to guide the readers or hearers of their Gospels to full faith and true Christian life. It was a man of Christian faith who wrote this Gospel, and he wrote, as 20:31 shows, to lead his readers to a sound and full faith and so to guide them reliably on the way to eternal life. The Gospel is a book that contains facts about Jesus, but it aims not primarily to give bare facts but to interpret what happened and so foster faith; it aims to bring glory to God and to build the Church by leading men to find their true life in Jesus Christ the Son of God.